The
Metis

The Canadian Issues Series

James Lorimer & Company has developed this series of original paperbacks to offer informed, up-to-date, critical introductions to key issues facing Canadians. Books are written specifically for the series by authors commissioned by the publisher on the basis of their expertise in a subject area and their ability to write for a general audience.

The 4" x 7" paperback format and cover design for the series offer attractive books at the lowest possible price. Special library hard-bound editions are also available. New titles are added to the series every spring and fall: watch for them in your local bookstore.

Already in print:

Misguided Missiles BY SIMON ROSENBLUM
Canada's Colonies BY KENNETH COATES
Police BY JOHN SEWELL
Ethics and Economics BY GREGORY BAUM AND DUNCAN CAMERON
The West BY J.F. CONWAY
Oil and Gas BY JAMES LAXER
Women and Work BY PAUL AND ERIN PHILLIPS
The New Canadian Constitution BY PAUL PHILLIPS
Out of Work BY CY GONICK
Rising Prices BY H. LUKIN ROBINSON
Industry in Decline BY RICHARD STARKS
Our Land: Native Rights in Canada BY DONALD PURICH

DONALD PURICH

The
Metis

James Lorimer & Company, Publishers
Toronto 1988

Copyright © 1988 by Donald Purich

All rights reserved. No part of this book may be reproduced or transmitted in any form or by any means, electronic or mechanical, including photocopying, or by any information storage or retrieval system, without permission in writing from the publisher.

Cover photograph: The Gabriel Dumont Institute

Canadian Cataloguing in Publication Data

Purich, Donald J., 1947-
   The Metis

(The Canadian issues series)
Bibliography: p.
Includes index.
ISBN 1-55028-052-X (bound) ISBN 1-55028-050-3 (pbk.)

1. Métis - History.- I. Title. II. Series:
Canadian issues series (Toronto, Ont.).

FC109.P87 1988 971'.00497 C88-093673-8
 E99.M693P87 1988

James Lorimer & Company, Publishers
Egerton Ryerson Memorial Building
35 Britain Street
Toronto, Ontario M5A 1R7

Printed and bound in Canada
6 5 4 3 2 1 88 89 90 91 92 93

Contents

Acknowledgements

First and foremost, I would like to thank Professor Richard Bartlett from the College of Law, University of Saskatchewan. Professor Bartlett, one of Canada's leading experts in native law, gave me advice on a number of questions. More important, he was kind enough to read a draft of this manuscript and provide me with a number of constructive suggestions for improving it.

Curtis Fahey, trade editor at James Lorimer & Co., also made a number of excellent suggestions for improving the manuscript. Catherine Marjoribanks copy-edited the manuscript and improved its style and flow.

In addition, a number of other people and institutions were most helpful.

The Gabriel Dumont Institute in Regina and its library staff were kind enough to give me access to their archives, The Metis Historical Collection. The Native Law Centre library at the University of Saskatchewan was a most valuable resource and its librarian, Linda Fritz, was very helpful. So too was the Government Documents Section of the Murray Memorial Library at the University of Saskatchewan. The Saskatoon *Star-Phoenix* library of news clippings was of considerable help in researching

Howard Adams' activities. Dianne Brydon, education liaison officer at the Diefenbaker Centre, helped me search out several matters in the Diefenbaker Archives. The Saskatchewan Archives Board and its staff were equally helpful.

Several people connected with Saskatchewan's Northern Development Advisory Committee provided me with information on current developments in northern Saskatchewan which seriously affect many of the Metis communities there. Those people included Richard Turkheim, secretary; Joanne Epp, senior research officer; and Dr. Walter Kupsch, council member.

Thomas R. Berger provided me with information on the lawsuit the Manitoba Metis Federation has launched. Clem Chartier and Larry Heinneman, from the Association of Metis and Non-Status Indians, gave me background information on constitutional matters. Gerald M. Morin and Murray Hamilton, at the time two Metis law students, provided me with information on other aspects of Metis political and social activity. Larry Chartrand, another Metis law student, gave me information on growing up and working in Alberta's Metis settlements. Cliff Supernault, executive director, Native Services Unit, Alberta Municipal Affairs, and his colleague Cameron Henry provided me with material on the Alberta Metis Settlements and kept me abreast of current developments regarding the settlements. Howard Leeson from the University of Regina also gave me information on the constitutional talks leading to the 1982 constitution.

Frank Tough from the Native Studies Department at the University of Saskatchewan briefed me on Metis languages, as did John Crawford from the University of

North Dakota. Howard Nixon, now assistant vice-president at the University of Saskatchewan, briefed me on Metis rights issues in Saskatchewan in the 1960s. Brenda Shular, of the University of Saskatchewan's Administrative Systems and Programming Department, helped with some computer applications.

A number of my colleagues at the College of Law, University of Saskatchewan, were of great assistance. Howard McConnell guided me through the intricacies of certain constitutional questions. Norman Zlotkin provided advice on constitutional issues and was also generous enough to read several draft pages of the manuscript dealing with the Constitution. Ken Norman provided advice on human rights questions.

A number of other people talked to me about the issues in this book, but asked that they not be publicly acknowledged. In other instances, because of the nature of their work or the negotiations they are involved in, I have felt it best not to mention their names. They will know who they are.

While many people provided me with assistance, the judgments, opinion and any errors are my own.

Finally, I would like to thank my wife, Karen Bolstad, who lived through the birthing process of this book.

Introduction

These are critical times for Canada's Metis people. Throughout the late 1970s and all of the 1980s the Metis have fought for constitutional recognition of certain rights: to be considered a distinct aboriginal society, to have a constitutionally protected land base and to be self-governing. That fight took them through the negotiations leading to the signing of the new Constitution in 1982, and through four subsequent constitutional conferences on aboriginal rights. While this process ended in a disappointing whimper with the collapse of the 1987 conference, the Metis have continued their campaign for constitutional protection. Along with other native groups they are pressing for the reopening of constitutional talks and are demanding amendments to the Meech Lake Accord which would recognize their status as distinct societies.

The Metis' campaign, moreover, has not been limited to the arena of national politics. As I write this book, the Manitoba Metis Federation is engaged in an historic legal battle in the province's courts. Arguing that they were deprived of nearly 2 million acres of prime Manitoba real estate by the unconstitutional acts of the federal and

Manitoba governments during the 1870s and 1880s, the Metis are asking for a comprehensive land settlement and monetary compensation. The outcome of this case will have momentous consequences for the Metis of western Canada, the province of Manitoba and the federal government. According to Thomas Berger, the counsel for the Metis, the case "constitutes the unfinished business of Canadian history" and will put "the conventional view of Canadian history on trial."

In Alberta, some Metis are engaged in an equally historic exercise. Stretching across northern Alberta and covering 1.25 million acres are eight Metis settlements, created by the provincial government in the 1930s as a relief program for destitute Metis. For decades these settlements were literally colonies run by the provincial bureaucracy. In 1984, however, a joint government-Metis committee recommended dramatic changes, and, to the surprise of many native leaders, Premier Peter Lougheed responded the following year with a resolution providing for the transfer of ownership of settlement lands from the government to the Metis, constitutional protection for those lands and a devolution of power to the settlements. Two years later the Metis presented a position paper to the Alberta government outlining their views on how Lougheed's resolution could be implemented, and some of the ideas in this paper were adopted in proposed legislation which the government revealed in June 1987. After almost fifty years of ruling the settlements with an iron fist, the government has announced that it plans to have the scheme in place in 1988. In view of the number of questions still unresolved between the parties, the government timetable might be unrealistic.

Constitutional questions, the Manitoba court case and Alberta's plans for its Metis settlements are only some of the complex issues facing the Metis today. Equally difficult are such questions as: Who are the Metis? Do they have aboriginal rights and, if so, what are those aboriginal rights? What forces determined the course of Metis history, and what does the future hold? These are the subjects of my book.

My own interest in the Metis dates back a long time. Growing up in a rural community on the Canadian prairies, I often heard the term "half-breed." Almost always it was used pejoratively and I never could understand why many adults were so contemptuous of these people.

It was with more than passing interest, therefore, that as a young adult in 1967 I listened to Howard Adams for the first time. The Berkeley-educated political activist identified himself as a "Half-breed" and was proud of it. He spoke out against the poverty and racism that were the lot of the Metis. He recalled the racism he had faced growing up in St. Louis, Saskatchewan, where the Metis were a significant part of the population, and he hinted at violence if things did not improve. He was a spellbinding speaker and today I can still remember much of his speech.

Several years later another Metis, Mederic McDougall, also of St. Louis, strongly supported me in my brief and unsuccessful political career. Mederic was not the orator that Howard Adams was, but in his own quiet way he introduced me to many aspects of "Metisism." My interest in the Metis continued as I pursued my career as a legal aid lawyer (working in several Metis communities) and after I obtained my current position as director of the University of Saskatchewan Native Law Centre.

Following publication of my previous book, *Our Land: Native Rights in Canada*, I was often asked if I was a native person. I am not, nor am I a white "bleeding heart liberal" so coloured by my political perceptions that I am unable to see both sides of the complex questions regarding the Metis. However, I do think that over the years I have gained some understanding of what the Metis seek and what issues Canada faces dealing with their claims. I have also come to the realization that the challenges and problems facing the Metis are not confined to the Metis themselves — they face all Canadians. Unfortunately, a great many people still live in ignorant bliss when it comes to understanding Metis issues. And when Canadians do try to come to grips with native issues, they often focus on Indian people alone. The Metis are truly "The Forgotten People," which, incidentally, was the title of a 1979 Native Council of Canada publication.

Recent events have made it clear that there is still a large gap to bridge between the aspirations of the Metis and what the majority of Canadians are prepared to concede. It is my hope that this book will in some small way help bridge that gap.

The Metis struggle for recognition and protection of their rights is the history of Canada. Every phase of Canadian history touched upon the Metis and in turn the Metis left their mark on most major historical events, including the rivalry between France and Britain for mastery of the continent, the struggle of the Catholic Church for a place in a Protestant country, the battle between rival groups for dominance of the fur trade in western Canada, the 1870 and 1885 rebellions, the formation of Manitoba, the devastation of the Great Depression on the Canadian prairies and the campaign for a new constitution in the 1980s. The Metis were the trail-blazers who led explorers, missionaries and traders westward and inland. They acted as middlemen between advancing European settlement and Indian bands. They acted as interpreters when treaties with Indians were negotiated. They brought the province of Manitoba into being. All of these contributions have often been ignored. Today, all the Metis seek is restitution and the recognition due to them for their role in building the nation.

Questions surrounding Metis rights are legally and historically complex; often there is no one correct interpretation, only assumptions and theories. Throughout the book I have tried to present all sides of the arguments and offer the reader my own conclusions.

This book mainly focuses, not on all mixed-blood people in Canada, but on the mixed-blood population of the Canadian west and north — the group to whom the term "Metis" is most often applied. The word "métis" is French and means "a child of different races, a mix." But the Metis are more than a French word; they are a people, and when they write of themselves many use the word "Metis" without the accent and with a capital "M". This is the form of the word I have chosen. In some documents and statutes that I quote the word "half-breed" is used. To remain faithful to the original I have not changed that term, which many Metis today find offensive. Occasionally, I have also used the term "Half-breed" with a capital "H". Some historians and social scientists use this word to denote Metis of English origin. I have used the word in those places in the text where I felt it was necessary to distinguish between English- and French-speaking Metis.

Donald Purich
Saskatoon
February, 1988

1

The Birth of the Metis Nation

St. Louis, Saskatchewan, population 452, is much like any other prairie village. A number of its businesses sport false fronts, which date from an era when prairie towns tried to display an image of economic prosperity that seldom accorded with reality. The town's only hotel, overlooking the South Saskatchewan River, resembles other small town prairie hotels in that it serves less as a place where out-of-town travellers can spend the night than as a place where locals can have a beer. All eyes turn on the stranger who walks in.

In other respects St. Louis is unusual. The town is in the heart of Saskatchewan's Metis belt. Batoche, often thought of as the capital of the Metis, is a mere thirty-minute drive over a country road still not entirely paved. A half-dozen other towns with significant Metis populations are within a 75-kilometre radius.

Saskatchewan is not the only province with Metis communities. Canada has a belt of Metis settlement that starts west of the Great Lakes, runs to Winnipeg, and then stretches through central and northern Manitoba, through Saskatchewan's parkland and into central Alberta. There are also substantial Metis populations in northern Alberta and Saskatchewan. Metis communities can be found in northern British Columbia, and a substantial Metis population exists in the Yukon and the western part of the Northwest Territories. In the latter, approximately five thousand Metis live in what will in future become Denendeh. (Denendeh is the name the Dene Indians — who are the major native group in the western NWT — use to describe their homeland. Today the name is widely used to describe the western NWT). Of course, there are people of mixed blood living throughout Canada.

The extent of Canada's Metis population is a matter for debate. In 1986, for the first time in over forty years, a national census tried to answer the question. People were asked if they considered themselves to be an aboriginal person and specifically if they considered themselves to be Inuit, status or registered Indian, non-status Indian or Metis. Unfortunately, the results did not prove conclusive. Many Indian communities boycotted the 1986 census and approximately 125,000 non-aboriginals misunderstood the question and identified themselves as aboriginals.

Prior to 1986, the Metis were enumerated in the 1941 census under the heading of "half-breed" and that census reported a Canadian total of 35,416 Metis, showing Alberta, Manitoba and Saskatchewan with the largest populations at approximately 9,000 Metis each. The accuracy of this figure is in serious doubt. The term "half-breed" had a derogatory meaning and many people had no desire to have themselves categorized in this way. In the 1960s the term gave way to the word Metis. In the early 1980s Metis spokespeople were estimating their population as high as 700,000. There have been other, lower estimates, with Statistics Canada estimating the Metis population in 1981 at 98,260.

Part of the problem in determining the Metis population is the difficulty in defining who the Metis are. The term has different meanings to different people. Thus two people with identical cultural and ethnic backgrounds might respond to the same census question in different ways.

Who Are the Metis?

The term Metis has been used in three different ways in Canada. It has often been used to include all native people who are not status Indians or Inuit. This is an incorrect usage; non-status Indians, while often lumped with the Metis, are essentially Indians who do not fall within the Indian Act definition of Indian or who, for one reason or another, were not enrolled in the Indian register. (By way of example: many full-blooded Indians in Newfoundland are not considered to be Indians under the Indian Act because at the time of union Ottawa and Newfoundland ignored the issue; in other provinces some Indian bands were often out hunting when treaties were signed and Indians enumerated, and therefore they never made it into the Indian register). While in many provinces non-status Indians and Metis have formed joint political organizations, it is the common struggle to gain recognition of their rights from Ottawa and the provinces that has drawn them together. Non-status Indians seek restoration of their Indian status and other rights accorded to their status kin. The Metis, on the other hand, seek recognition as a distinct people.

Non-status Indians, and to a lesser extent the Metis, have been affected by 1985 changes to The Indian Act, commonly referred to as the Bill C-31, which allowed persons who had surrendered their Indian status (in order to marry or gain an education or employment) to regain it. It is estimated that approximately 75,000 non-status Indians and Metis may qualify; however, some people calculate that as many as 300,000 people may be affected. In some instances, Indians who lost their status called themselves Metis, and have now applied for reinstatement. And for reasons outlined later in the book, some Metis were allowed to register as status Indians. If they later gave up or lost their Indian status, they may in some instances be able to reacquire it. In short, Bill C-31 will have some effect on Metis numbers.

The term Metis is also used to describe all mixed-blood people, including children of modern-day intermarriages, many of whom have been assimilated into the mainstream of Canadian society. Generally, most Metis organizations are prepared to recognize these people as Metis on condition that they identify themselves as Metis. Thus, in part, whether one is a Metis can be a matter of self-definition.

Most often, the term Metis is used to refer to the descendants of the historic Metis — that is, those whose origin can be traced back to the Red River in the early 1800s. These are the people, now located mainly in the prairie provinces and the north, who joined together to fight the Hudson's Bay Company (HBC) and who in 1869 formed a government to negotiate their entry into the Canadian federation. They also formed a culture which was a unique blend of Indian and European cultures and developed their own unique languages — patois, Michif and Bungi. The last of these, Bungi, a combination of Orkney Scottish and Cree, was the language developed by the English-speaking Metis. It has largely vanished, being spoken only in a few small communities in Manitoba. Patois is a French dialect — French with an Indian influence. Michif, often considered by linguists not as a dialect but as a true language, is a mixture of French, Cree, Ojibwa and English. In the *Michif Dictionary*, a North Dakota scholar, John C. Crawford, describes Michif as:

> ...dominated by two [languages], French and Cree, and in a pattern of combination which is most unusual and in its way very rigorous. The structure of the noun phrase, names of things and the words which go with them, is clearly French, even to preserving French gender and the rules of sound combination, whereas verbs in Michif show the range and complexity of affixation that characterizes Algonquian languages, and which are in fact, Plains Cree.

Patois and Michif are still spoken in parts of the prairies.

In addition to language, the Metis developed many other unique cultural characteristics. One of these was dress, a central feature of which was "L'Assomption Sash" (named after the town in Quebec where it had its origins). This colourful sash, worn by many (but definitely not all) Metis in the 1800s was not just a piece of colourful clothing; it had many functional purposes as well. The sash had fringed ends — the fringes served as an emergency sewing kit when the Metis were out on the buffalo hunt. A key, which opened a trunk containing all their valuable possessions, was sometimes tied to the fringes. The sash also served as a first-aid kit, a washcloth and towel, and as an emergency bridle and saddle blanket when the Metis were out on the hunt. Recognizing the importance of the sash, many Metis organizations today have started to award the "Order of the Sash" to individuals who have made outstanding contributions to the Metis cause.

When they settled in the Red River Valley and later on the banks of the Saskatchewan River the Metis established long narrow individual plots (a narrow frontage along the river which ran back for a long distance) much in the manner of French settlers in New France. These lots were usually 2 miles long and 792 feet wide, comprising some 200 acres. Haylots, woodlots and pastures were located behind the riverlots.

Many of the Metis adopted the Catholic faith. In 1987 the Metis sought to persuade the Pope to come to Batoche, emphasizing how much their lives were intertwined with the Church. At the time a spokesperson for the Metis National Council, Marc LeClair, stated that the Metis system of landholding was based on the parishes:

> If you look at downtown Winnipeg and the Red River area, it was clusters of parishes all the way along....The church was the central component of Metis society....The parish in Batoche was the central meeting place, where political and social activity took place. In the end [the church at Batoche] was the last stronghold when the troops closed in and where the Metis surrendered.

Of course, these are historical generalizations. It should be borne in mind that not all Metis were hunters, not all wore sashes, many spoke no patois and some were not Catholics. Some became successful businessmen. Others renounced their roots and claimed to be French.

The Metis themselves have wrestled with the question of their identity. The Metis National Council defines Metis as the following: all persons who can show they are descendants of persons considered as Metis under the 1870 Manitoba Act; all persons who can show they are descendants of persons considered as Metis under the Dominion Lands Act of 1879 and 1883; and all other persons who can produce proof of aboriginal ancestry and who have been accepted as Metis by the Metis community. The first two categories clearly restrict Metis to those people whose origins are in the Red River valley. The last category would allow considerable room for self-identification.

The MNC definition has been criticized by many groups as being too narrow and focusing too much on western Canada. A number of people have argued that there are disadvantaged people of partially native origin who are not status Indians and who were not considered Metis under the Manitoba Act or the Dominion Lands Act. Because of their Indian origin they should have some aboriginal rights. The MNC definition is limited to those mixed-blood people to whom the federal government made promises in the 1870s and 1880s, promises which, the Metis allege, were never fulfilled.

In the end, the courts may have a major say in defining Metis. Someday, as part of a lands claim case, they might have to rule whether mixed-blood people have aboriginal rights and, if so, which people qualify for such rights. And in the litigation commenced by the Manitoba Metis Federation, the courts might have to decide which mixed-blood people qualify for compensation for broken government promises.

The difficulty even the Metis have in defining their membership is illustrated by a dispute which arose in Alberta in 1987. The leadership of the southern zone of the Metis Association of Alberta complained that the association's membership criteria were too slack — any Metis member of the association was allowed to take a sworn statement that an applicant for membership was a Metis. One association member, Aurele Dumont, offered a solution to the problem. He called for a national membership deadline for those wanting to qualify as Metis. An extensive advertising campaign, sponsored by the federal government, would ensure nobody was missed. Without such precautions, he feared a flood of new applicants for Metis status would result from the announcement of any land claims settlement.

His proposal has been supported by other Metis leaders and organizations, including the Metis National Council, which has called for a federal enumeration of Metis. The federal government has ignored the plan, arguing that a census is sufficient.

Defining "Metis" is not merely an academic question. If land claims settlements between the Metis and governments are reached, it will be important to know who can live on the land and, more important, who can partake in the income earned by the land. If Metis governments become reality it will be necessary to know who can participate in those governments. The Metis are claiming the right to do the defining. Essentially, their definition includes not only the Metis originating in the Red River area but also any person who considers himself a Metis and is recognized as such by the community.

The involvement of the Metis in defining themselves is crucial — the less than happy experience of the federal government in trying to define "Indians" by way of the Indian Act should be an example. Yet, while Metis organizations may help develop general criteria, the process begins with an individual's choice to identify himself or herself as a Metis.

The Birth of the Metis People

The growth of a mixed-blood population is by no means unique to Canada. In many South and Central American countries the mixed-blood people form a significant part of the population. In Ecuador, 45 per cent of the country's 8 million people and its largest racial group is *Mestizo*, the Spanish-American term for mixed-blood people. What makes the mixed-blood population of Canada unique is that they developed a distinct cultural and political identity. They did not seek to be Indians nor, as in many South American countries, did they aspire to become white.

More than one historian has joked about the Metis people having their origin nine months after the first Europeans landed in the Americas. There is some truth to the joke. People of mixed-blood were noted in Nova Scotia in the early 1600s.

The birth of the Metis people remains to a large extent a matter for historical speculation. There was no journalist or historian to witness the first contact between European men and Indian women. Nor for that matter are there many records of any kind documenting those early encounters. Therefore, as with the social histories of other peoples, assumptions have to be made.

That liaisons arose between Indian women and white men is not surprising. It is not difficult to imagine the sexual frustrations of European soldiers and traders after weeks spent in transatlantic journeys. In the early days of European exploration there were very few, if any, white women living in the Americas. European observers noted that such associations were not frowned upon by Indian leaders in the early days of contact. Many chiefs saw it as a honour for a white man to establish a liaison with a woman from the tribe — such a man could be a valuable commercial contact for an Indian band. Also noted by some observers was the Indian custom of accepting illegitimate children into their society without regarding their origin as a degrading blemish. Perhaps these circumstances may explain why Indian women were willing to enter into relationships with white men. Of course, Indian bands often had no choice but to accept the children of such unions, since the families were frequently abandoned by the trader father.

Two European groups had an impact on the growth of a mixed-blood people in Canada — the Scots and the French. These two groups were very different, yet both left their distinct imprint on the Metis nation. In many ways the French influence was the more important of the two. Quebec has historically supported the Metis cause and even today the Metis often look to Quebec for support.

The rulers of New France believed that Indians were savages who needed to be civilized and Christianized. But they also believed — and this theme runs through all of the King's orders and grants of trading rights — that the natives and French colonists should merge into a single race. Samuel de Champlain was instructed by the French Crown in 1612 to "...call them [the Indians], have them instructed, provoke, and move them to the knowledge and service of God and by the light of the Catholic faith and religion...." Benefits awaited the Indians who came to the faith. The charter granted to the Company of One Hundred Associates in 1627 provided that "...converted natives...will be considered...as...French citizens and as such may live in France." In addition, Champlain promised the Huron Indians that French men would go into the country to marry their daughters, and Louis XIV instituted a King's Gift, a sum of money, to encourage mixed marriages. A common practice of French traders was to send young French boys to live with the Indians to learn their ways; Champlain himself sent a boy to live with the Algonquins. This practice sped up the process of mixing of the races.

Along with official encouragement there were many practical reasons for the French to mingle with the Indians. In the early days New France was a thin line of settlement stretching along the St. Lawrence River. Colonists were never far from the wilderness and were in close contact with the Indian people. Hunting was necessary to supplement the food produced by the colony's farms and such expeditions often took the colonists deep into Indian country. In addition, since New France was a trading colony, it was incumbent on many of the settlers to meet with the Indian tribes in order to make a living.

As a result, by the early 1700s there was a mixed-blood population in the vicinity of New France. Most of the mixed-blood people were adopted by Indian tribes. This was a common phenomenon in the early settlements of eastern Canada and the United States. Many Algonquin tribes called these people "wissakodewinmi," meaning burned stick, a phrase that eventually led to the French term "bois-brûlé" (burnt wood) to describe the Metis. It was only after the French traders started their westward expansion that the mixed-blood people began to develop a separate identity.

The process of western expansion began early on. Champlain was forced to choose between Indian allies — there were the Iroquois to the south and southwest, and the Hurons, Algonquins and Ottawas to the north and west (the Ottawa valley-Georgian Bay area). By choosing the latter group he antagonized the Iroquois, and the ensuing French-Iroquois wars forced New France to expand in the direction of the Great Lakes. It is believed that by the 1670s to 1680s some French traders had reached the west shore of Lake Superior. There is even speculation that by the 1690s some French traders may have reached as far as the shores of Lake Winnipeg. While warfare in the 1680s with the Iroquois forced many of the traders to return home to fight, by the early 1700s they were back and had established a number of posts in the region west of present-day Thunder Bay. Some historians estimate that in the 1700s there were probably 50 communities west of the Chicago-Green Bay area populated by French mixed-blood traders and their families.

While trade required them to travel frequently, these people established permanent communities where they grew wheat, peas and potatoes.

Western expansion continued in the 18th century. In 1731 Pierre Gaultier de Varennes de La Vérendrye was commissioned by the King of France to find the western ocean. By the 1740s one of his sons had reached the foot of the Rocky Mountains. The king did not provide La Vérendrye with any funds to finance this expedition; he had to pay for it by trading with the Indians and to this end he established a number of trading posts. In order to gain the loyalty of the Indians, he continued the practice of placing young men with Indian tribes so as to learn their language and ways. He even placed two of his sons for adoption with the Cree.

Shortly after his foray into the prairies La Vérendrye was deprived of his western trade monopoly and a number of other Montreal traders were given franchises. By the 1750s French traders had built several trading posts across the prairies, including The Pas (in north-central Manitoba) and Fort à la Corne (near present-day Prince Albert).

The outbreak of war between France and England in the 1750s forced many of the traders to return to New France to fight against the English. Some of them, however, remained in the west among the Indian tribes. They became the freemen typified by Louis Primeau, an illiterate braggart and master of Indian languages, who went to work for the Hudson's Bay Company in 1764 but quickly left after finding the English too stifling for his liking. Primeau allegedly did his share in the establishment of a mixed-blood population.

The Battle for Furs

Following the French defeat on the Plains of Abraham in 1759, a number of Montreal traders decided to resume their western operations. Primarily they worked as independent traders, but in the late 1760s and early 1770s, realizing that by joining together they could be much more effective in transporting goods to the west, they began to form partnerships. One of the most important partnerships, the North West Company (NWC), was formed in the late 1770s and was an alliance of French and Scottish interests; many of the Montreal traders were Scots, while most of the people in the field were French. At first, the NWC faced several competitors, but by 1804, when it took over the XY Company, it had successfully swallowed up all its Montreal-based rivals.

The NWC traders followed the patterns already established by their French predecessors when it came to dealing with the Indians. They made a point of learning their languages and customs. Many of the traders wintered with the Indians. Unlike their HBC counterparts, they also started settlements. And they had no hesitation in taking Indian wives.

An Indian wife was crucial to commercial success and survival in the west. The heads of the NWC posts encouraged such marriages. An Indian wife ensured the trader contact with a tribe and also provided skills necessary for survival.

Peter C. Newman, in his *Company of Adventurers*, states that these liaisons were not always voluntary: "French traders played dangerous games by carrying off young Indian women against their will, forcing them to share their beds...."

The NWC's policy of encouraging relationships with Indian women was perhaps too successful. In 1805 Alexander Henry, a NWC post manager, estimated that there were 368 wives and 569 children for 1,090 traders. In his own post he had 36 traders, 27 wives and 67 children. By this time the NWC was experiencing financial difficulties. These pressures forced the company to order that women and children could no longer live in the posts and were the sole responsibility of the traders.

The birth of the HBC predated that of the NWC by at least a century and had much to do with two dissatisfied French fur traders, Pierre-Esprit Radisson and Médard Chouart, Sieur Des Groseilliers. These two adventurers were keen on exploring Hudson Bay and mounted several expeditions into that area. However, New France's governor, afraid that exploration and trading in the region of Hudson Bay might shift the focus of the fur trade away from the St. Lawrence River, forbade the two men to carry out further explorations in the region. In response, Radisson and Groseilliers went to the English. The year 1665 found them in London convincing King Charles II of the trade prospects in the Hudson Bay area. Charles began discussing the possibility of an expedition to the Bay and this discussion piqued the interest of Prince Rupert, soldier, inventor and entrepreneur. The prince put together a commercial syndicate which on June 3, 1668, sent the ship *Nonsuch* to Hudson Bay. It returned a year later loaded with furs. The success of the syndicate prompted it to press for a royal charter granting a monopoly on trade into Hudson Bay. This was granted on May

2, 1670, when the Hudson's Bay Company, as it was called, was given dominion over some 3 million square miles.

The company thus created was to have a long and successful career (today it runs a chain of department stores, among other businesses). Over the three centuries of its existence it survived French military attacks, fought off its Montreal-based rivals and swallowed its most prominent opponent, the NWC, in 1821. But the HBC was more than a mere commercial enterprise. It was the government of the west — it made laws and enforced them, minted coins and issued a calendar dating from its formation. In this capacity it had a profound influence, not only in shaping western Canada, but also in creating Metis nationalism.

For almost a century after its founding the company did not venture out of the Bay. It was content to sit there and force the Indians to come to it. In fact, for a long time HBC men were prohibited from travelling inland unless they had permission from company headquarters in London. The few HBC traders who actually received permission to go inland, like Henry Kelsey in 1690, built no forts and left no sign of their presence.

Only intense competition from the Quebec traders forced the company to move inland. In 1773 the governing committee of the HBC in London, England, authorized the establishment of an interior post. Cumberland House (in north-east Saskatchewan) was established the next year; subsequently, many other posts were built across the prairies.

From the first, the HBC, unlike the NWC, discouraged interaction between its employees and the Indians. A military atmosphere prevailed in most of the posts. Changes in shift, meals and bedtime were signalled by bells. Attendance at Sunday morning worship was a must. Letters home were censored. At one point in the company's history all business between the HBC and Indians took place through a trading window, with traders barred from talking with their Indian clients. Liaisons with Indian women meant imprisonment or pay loss and in some posts such indiscretions were punished by whippings. Getting venereal disease meant a loss of one month's pay.

A hundred years after the company's creation the strictures were still in place. In 1768 Andrew Graham, who served as chief factor and governor of a number of posts in his twenty-six-year career with the company, ordered that "no...person is allowed to have any correspondence with the Natives without the Chief's orders, not even to go into an Indian tent and the Natives are not permitted to come within the forts but when their business requires." When one John Butler, another company manager, wanted to send his son to live with the Indians so he could learn the language, the London managing committee replied, "We do hereby order you [Butler] not to suffer him [his son] or any other Person to be absent from his duty on such pretence...."

Many of these rules governing white-Indian contact were impossible to enforce and were openly flouted. Some of the rules ignored the realities of a fur-trading operation. The rules and restrictions mostly originated with the company's management in London; these men knew little about the country in which their company operated, and most had no interest in learning anything about Canada. Enforcement of the rules depended on the local managers, who often defied the rules themselves. As early as 1682 the governing committee in London threatened not to pay salaries to the chief factors who let Indian women into their posts and who tolerated infractions of the "law of God." Some officers strictly obeyed this rule and established their liaisons outside the fort. Relationships with Indian women were common in spite of the rules. Even Andrew Graham succumbed. By the end of his twenty-six-year tenure with the HBC he had had at least one child — a daughter — by an Indian mistress. He begged the London management committee to be allowed to bring his daughter to England — the committee refused.

Still, HBC policies on Indian-white interaction were not entirely unsuccessful. Although many of the company's employees were Scots from the Orkney Islands, the mixed-blood population resulting from Scottish-Indian unions was not as great as that resulting from French-Indian ones. In the 1820s to 1840s the Half-breeds equalled the Metis; however, by the 1860s the Metis significantly outnumbered the Half-breeds. The Half-breeds were also more likely to marry into the Metis group than vice versa. And perhaps because of the reserved manner of their Scottish fathers, the Half-breeds were less nationalistic than the Metis. It was the Metis, morally supported by the French in Quebec, who led the events of 1869-70. Today the distinction between the two groups has largely vanished.

The Awakening of Metis Nationalism

There are people who question the importance of the fur trade in the rise of the Metis. Duke Redbird, a former president of the Ontario Metis and Non-Status Indian Association, in his book *We Are the Metis, A Metis View of the Development of a Native Canadian People*, concludes:

> The most common assumption with the early Metis is that the conflict between the North West Company and the Hudson's Bay Company created the first sense of identity among the Metis....That the Metis existence is a result of human relationships and not political machinations is largely ignored by most writers. The birth of the Metis came about as a result of a "participation mystique," a desire of people wanting to get together. It had no intentional political function even though the result created political and cultural changes that played a major role in the history of Canada.

He further contends that the first Metis in the Red River were Metis who moved from eastern Canada. They intermarried with local Indians and formed a unique people.

In part, Redbird's comments reflect the feeling among many Metis that historians (mostly non-native) generally tend to overemphasize the role of the fur traders in the formation of the Metis nation and to downplay the role of the Indians. There is more than a grain of truth to this view. Until recently, much of the historical and social science research on the Metis has tended to focus on the traders. But Indian nations were just as important as Europeans in shaping Metis culture. Their traditions and languages are an integral part of Metis culture and their influence is such that the Metis identify themselves as a native people and not as non-natives.

Among the Europeans, moreover, the traders were not the only people who contributed to the rise of the Metis — the influence of the Catholic Church was also critical. On the prairies, the first Catholic church was built in St. Boniface in 1818 to serve the growing French population, mostly Metis, who were settling in the area. The Church had a vision of a French Catholic west and the Metis were an important element of that vision. Hence, a close relationship developed between the Church and the Metis. The Church encouraged the Metis in the use of French and helped them become a united group. Catholic priests served as Metis advisors during the rebellions of 1869 and 1885. They helped the Metis draft petitions and carried them to Ottawa. They tried to protect the Metis from unscrupulous speculators. In many ways, the Catholic clergy served as the Metis' lawyers in the 1800s.

Yet, when all is said and done, we must return to the HBC as the force that turned the Metis into a cohesive political unit. The company stubbornly maintained an aloof attitude towards the Metis, and even worse, discriminated against them in a variety of ways. Motivated by racism and a desire to protect its trading monopoly, the company gave the Metis something to hate. More important, its conduct united them in a common cause — the struggle against the restrictive and discriminatory rules of the HBC.

2
Early Struggles

By the early 1800s, conflict between the Metis and the HBC was unavoidable. First, there was a struggle over the fur trade. The HBC was faced with stiff competition from its main rival, the Montreal-based NWC, which relied extensively on Metis traders. Then there was the matter of the Metis settlements. While the Metis were a nomadic people, they did establish settlements as a base to which they could return after a hunting or trading trip. The HBC viewed these communities as the vanguard of a more populous, settled society which would not be under its control and would interfere with the fur trade.

The settlements began to spring up in the late 1700s and early 1800s near NWC posts and near the junction of important river trading-routes. Often the NWC encouraged the Metis, many of whom were its employees, to settle near its posts. Some historians estimate that in the early 1800s there were between four thousand and five thousand Metis in western Canada. Other historians more conservatively estimate the population to have been closer to five hundred Metis in the 1820s. Politically, the settlements were important because they brought the Metis together into a community where they could discuss common concerns and take action. Of course, this also made them more susceptible to exploitation by the NWC.

The first Metis settlements were at Fort William (now Thunder Bay) and at the junction of the Red and Assiniboine Rivers (now Winnipeg). Other early settlements in the Manitoba-North Dakota area included Pembina, Hair Hills and Deer Lake. Later Metis settlements were founded in what is today Edmonton (originally called Fort des Prairies), and at other Alberta locations, such as Lac La Biche, Lac Ste.-Anne and Lesser Slave Lake. Many of these were formed near trading posts. Settlements in Saskatchewan, like those in the Batoche area and in the Cypress Hills, followed. All of these settlements predated the arrival of European settlers. This is an important factor in Metis claims today; while the Metis may not have occupied these settlements since time immemorial, they can claim occupation prior to European colonization.

The most important Metis communities were those in the Red River Valley, an area that was conducive to settlement. Game and fish were plentiful. The soil lent itself to cultivation and the surrounding marsh areas provided foraging grounds for horses. Gradually, log cabins, with walls of whitish clay and roofs of bark, were built. Wild rice was harvested and small plots of wheat and potatoes were grown. Historians disagree on when the Metis, particularly those in the Red River area, started cultivating the soil. Some feel that it was in the early 1800s; others suggest that the Metis did not start tilling the soil until the 1850s.

While the Metis engaged in agriculture, for decades their most important source of food was the buffalo. The buffalo hunt was not only a means of obtaining food, it was also a social event. Significantly, the hunt taught the Metis military and organizational skills which would prove to be invaluable in later struggles.

The Buffalo Hunt

The scene: hundreds of men charging at full gallop across the prairie, screaming at the top of their voices, their red sashes flying, guns blazing, group flags barely visible in the storm of dust raised by thousands of buffalo and horse hooves. Soon a hundred buffalo have fallen. Each hunter leaves a marker on the buffalo he has shot. The hunt stops; guns are put away; the dust hovers for hours. The women and children leave the teepees at the campsite to skin the carcasses and cut up the meat. The men sit around the campfire reliving the day's events. Such was the buffalo hunt.

The hunt involved organizing hundreds of men, women, children, carts and horses for westward journeys extending hundreds of kilometres; on the trip back tons of buffalo meat and hides had to be carried. At the time there was no commercial or military activity of that magnitude in western Canada. The buffalo hunt provided the Metis with an impressive organizational structure and by 1820 was a permanent feature of Red River life.

In his 1856 book, *The Red River Settlement: Its Rise, Progress, and Present State; With Some Account of Native Races and its General History to the Present Day*, Alexander Ross describes travelling from the Red River with 1,630 Metis in the 1840 hunt. After three days of travel through the dust raised by the 1,240 carts used in the hunt, camp was made and the first organizational meeting for the hunt held. Ten captains were chosen, one of whom was to be the senior captain. Ten soldiers and ten guides were assigned to each captain. Guides were responsible for the camp flag which remained raised until it was time to settle for the night. During the actual hunt the soldiers and even the captain were under the command of the guides. At the end of the day the captains took charge. The carts were placed in a circle within which the tents were set up.

The hunt was governed by detailed rules. At one council meeting the following rules were established: no hunting on Sunday; no one to lag behind, dash ahead or break off from his group; no one to begin shooting until the order to fire is given; each captain and his soldiers to establish night patrols to guard the camp. The following punishments were prescribed for breaching rules: first offence, saddle and bridle cut up; second offence, offender's coat cut up; and third offence, public flogging. Theft resulted in the offender being put in the middle of the camp and publicly called a thief three times. At many of these meetings the assembled hunters had to vote on these rules to make them binding.

The 1840 hunt, which began in early June, covered 250 miles in 19 days before the first buffalo were sighted. By the time the hunt ended on August 17 it had captured over a million pounds of meat and hides, all of which had to be transported back to the Red River settlements. The meat fed Metis families, white colonists and fur traders. The Metis did a brisk business in supplying first the NWC, and after 1821 the HBC, with dried buffalo meat and pemmican. Once back at the Red River the Metis returned to their individual riverlots to take up other activities including gardening, farming, fishing, harvesting wild rice, building carts and making clothing, collecting lime, limestone, maple sugar, salt and seneca root.

Not all Metis returned to the Red River after the annual buffalo hunt. Some, known as the *hivernants*, chose to remain on the prairies setting up semi-permanent cabins and settlements. Roughly thirty such settlements have been found in Alberta, Saskatchewan and Montana. As the buffalo diminished in number, the Metis had to travel farther west to find the animal. This in turn meant more Metis settlements. By the 1850s and 1860s buffalo hunts were being organized from settlements in the Cypress Hills, in the St. Albert-Edmonton area and in the Batoche area.

The Plains Indians also hunted the buffalo and as the herds declined conflict errupted between the Indians and Metis. In the mid-1840s and 1850s the Metis successfully fought the Sioux for control of the hunt in what is today North Dakota. The Sioux retaliated by setting prairie fires which drove the buffalo away and kept the Metis out. Eventually, the Metis and the Sioux concluded a peace treaty.

A decade later the fight moved north. In the 1850s and 1860s the Metis battled the Cree in the Qu'Appelle Valley over the right to hunt buffalo. The Metis were successful; by the 1860s they completely dominated the pemmican market and became the most important suppliers of that commodity for the HBC.

Of course, not all Metis took part in the buffalo hunt.

Duke Redbird estimates that the proportion of Metis involved in the hunt was less than one-third. But for those Metis who did take part, particularly those in the Red River area where the hunt was centred, it was an important element in shaping them into a cohesive political and military unit.

Conflict at Red River

By the time Thomas Douglas, Earl of Selkirk, decided to settle some of his impoverished Scottish countrymen in the Red River area, there were a number of thriving Metis communities there. Yet, in what would become a characteristic pattern of dealing with native people, nobody consulted the Metis about the establishment of a new settlement in their midst.

In the mid-1700s landlords in the Scottish Highlands began forcing some of their small tenant-farmers off the land because they found they could make much more money grazing sheep. In the ten-year period between 1809 and 1819 some 450,000 acres were taken away from tenants, whose families had in some cases farmed the land for centuries. They started to look for places to settle in the Scottish lowlands and in the Americas.

Selkirk was concerned about the social unrest that might follow such a migration into Scottish and English cities, especially since these people were often ill-suited to urban life. At the same time he wanted to make sure that these displaced farmers remained British subjects (he had great fears of his Scottish compatriots enriching the newly formed United States of America). His answer — form new colonies. Before turning his gaze towards Red

River, he established colonies near Lake St. Clair in Upper Canada and in Prince Edward Island. Later he entered into discussions with the HBC, in which he and his two brothers-in-law had a controlling interest, for the purchase of land on which to build a third colony. These discussions eventually led to the purchase of 116,000 acres in the Red River area. The price was ten shillings.

The company saw advantages in having a colony in the Red River area because it meant a source of local Scottish manpower for the trading posts and for a militia. Selkirk, in fact, promised that the colony would provide the company with two hundred men a year. A farming colony, if successful, also meant a reliable local supply of food. And a colony along the Red River area would interfere with the NWC's operations — NWC posts were located on the land ceded, and the Red River was situated in the middle of that company's route between Montreal and its western trading posts.

The NWC, for its part, saw the colony as a grave threat, partly for the reasons just mentioned but also because of its fear that the Red River colony would be the first of many settlements. More settlements would mean the end of the fur trade, which would mean the end of the company. A Canadian partner of the NWC told the company's London partners that the colony would be "fatal to the very existence of their trade." The company did its best to dissuade the settlers from leaving Scotland. One of the company's agents wrote in the *Inverness Journal* that, "...even if they (the emigrants) escape the scalping knife, they will be subject to constant alarm and terror. Their habitations, their crops, their cattle will be destroyed, and they will find it impossible to exist in the country...." The emigrants were not deterred — few of the tenant farmers could read.

In September 1811 two shiploads of colonists left for the Red River. After wintering at York Factory, the first colonists, under the command of Miles Macdonell, reached the junction of the Red and Assiniboine Rivers in August 1812. A month later Macdonell held a formal ceremony marking the establishment of the colony. A fancy tent was set up; Macdonell read the Act of Cession whereby the HBC had given up the land, while six guns boomed outside. Drinks followed. The ceremony was attended by two NWC officers and eighteen Metis and Indians.

Initially, many Metis worked for the colony. They supplied game (mostly buffalo) and garden produce. There is evidence to suggest that many of the colonists would have starved the first year had it not been for the Metis' assistance.

The Metis eventually turned against the colony for two reasons. First, the colony's governor, Macdonell, was less than tactful in his dealings with the Metis and did not give any recognition to the fact that the Metis settlements predated his. Totally lacking in diplomatic skills, he berated those who dared question him or make suggestions. It was an odd approach for someone who was in fact intruding on someone else's territory.

As well, the Metis were goaded by the NWC into fighting the colony. In a speech to the Metis a NWC official, Alexander Macdonell (no relation to the colony's governor), said:

...these people [the colonists] have been spoiling fair lands which belong to you and the Bois-Brûlés....They have no right. They have been driving away the buffalo. You will soon be poor and miserable. But we will drive them away if the Indians do not; for the North West Company and the Bois-Brûlés are one.

The NWC turned to Cuthbert Grant, one of the more influential Metis, to lead the campaign against the Selkirk settlement. Grant lived in Pembina, which later proved to be on the American side of the border. Known by such names as Captain of the Metis, Captain General of the Half-breeds and Warden of the Plains, Grant was not typical of the people of Pembina. He was a well-dressed gentlemen often seen in a frock coat, breeches, beaver top hat and boots; in contrast, his fellow townspeople wore handmade clothes from skins and furs which they themselves had harvested. Grant, the son of a wealthy Scottish trader of the NWC, acquired his sophisticated ways during an eleven-year absence from Red River spent at school in Scotland and in eastern Canada. Upon his return from school he worked for the NWC and became a leading member of the Metis community. He was articulate and educated, but still retained his Metis culture. He could ride and shoot as well as any man, danced a mean jig and could down a bottle of rum in one sitting. He was also a real ladies' man, with five wives in the space of a decade.

Grant, who genuinely believed that the Red River colony was a threat to the Metis way of life, proved invaluable in the NWC's campaign to destroy the settlement. Under his leadership, the Metis resorted to many tricks, one of which was to deprive the colony of one of its sources of food by running buffalo out of the area. Those Metis who did not join the battle were dealt with by the NWC. Metis who worked for the colonists or who supplied food to them were severely punished — one had his horses permanently seized for supplying the colony.

The colony's governor, Miles Macdonnell, fought back in characteristic fashion. Even though his people were outnumbered, he did not try to negotiate. Instead he ordered, in 1814, that no Metis were to run buffalo out of the area, and then proceeded to seize their pemmican. Some of this pemmican was destined for the NWC and some was the Metis' food supply. He also seized pemmican belonging to the NWC which had been stored at Fort La Souris.

The NWC urged the Metis to retaliate. They did. Led by Grant, they spent the summer of 1815 burning the settlers' crops, stealing their cattle and machinery, and destroying improvements such as fences and buildings. Although the raids did not drive the colonists away, in early 1816 Grant seemed confident of victory: "It is hoped that we shall come off with flying colours and never see any of them again in the Colonizing way in Red River...."

The next round of battle came in May 1816 when the Metis captured the HBC's pemmican boats on the Qu'Appelle River and then plundered the company's Brandon House, intending to move the captured pemmican to Lake Winnipeg so it could be shipped to NWC posts on the prairies (the Saskatchewan River, which flows to Hudson Bay via the north end of Lake Winnipeg, was a major water route into western Canada). To get to Lake Winnipeg they had to skirt the Selkirk colony. Their plan was to travel down the Assiniboine (which flowed to the colony) and to leave the river ten miles upstream from the colony, and then to travel overland to Lake Winnipeg. Wet banks and marshy land made this plan impossible. The result — the Metis were only three miles away from the colony when they finally started their overland trek. The new governor of the colony, Robert Semple, on hearing of the proximity of the Metis, took a party of twenty men to find out what they were up to and to assert his authority over the area. When the governor sighted the Metis he saw only the advance party of 15 men. Several farmers warned him that a much larger party of Metis were following, but he did not wait. He decided to make clear to the Metis who was in charge.

The two groups met in a shady group of trees known as Seven Oaks in the late afternoon of June 19. Grant sent a messenger offering the governor a choice — either surrender or be fired upon. The messenger and Semple spoke briefly and began to argue. Semple tried to grab the messenger's gun and reins; the messenger fell from his horse and started to run; shots were exchanged. Both sides went into action. By nightfall twenty-one settlers, including Semple himself, and one Metis were dead.

The Battle of Seven Oaks did not sound the death-knell for the colony. Military reinforcements arrived to protect the settlers and legal proceedings were taken against the NWC. Lord Selkirk himself arrived in the colony bringing more troops. He entered into immediate negotiations with the local Ojibwa, Cree and Assiniboine Indians with the purpose of reaching treaties with them to ensure that the Indians would side with the colony.

A warrant was issued for Grant's arrest. Grant voluntarily went to Montreal to face criminal charges, including murder. After being released on bail he returned to the west. The court proceedings against him were abandoned; in fact, he was soon hired by the HBC.

While the colony survived the Battle of Seven Oaks, so did the Metis, now a stronger political and military unit. This was the first time the Metis had united to fight a common threat and they had obviously achieved a degree of military success. According to some observers, it was during the battle that the Metis first flew their flag, a horizontal figure eight on a blue background. The Metis battle spirit displayed at Seven Oaks was immortalized in a song written by Pierre Falcon, Grant's brother-in-law and companion in arms:

> Ah, would you had seen those Englishmen,
> And the Bois-Brûlés a-chasing them
> One by one we did them destroy
> While our Bois-Brûlés uttered shouts of joy

The HBC Wins — and Loses

While the NWC put up a valiant fight, the high cost of transporting goods presented another obstacle. Not only did trading goods have to come from Montreal, much of the way by canoe, but furs had to return the same way. In 1821 the NWC merged with the HBC, to form one giant trading firm with a monopoly over the fur trade in the west. In fact, the monopoly was extended by a twenty-one year license to include the Arctic and the Pacific coast.

But the HBC's actions were such as to ensure that its monopoly would not last long.

The company went out of its way to aggravate the local Metis and Indian population. Even before it regained its monopoly in 1821 the HBC's treatment of its Metis employees (whether of Scottish or French descent) left much to be desired. It paid its Metis employees about half what its Scottish employees received for doing the same work. At one point in its history the company paid its lower echelon employees a maximum of ten pounds; a Metis employee doing the same work would make a maximum of six pounds. Mostly, the Metis worked as labourers and few ever rose above the rank of postmaster or trader. Management positions — whether at the level of clerk or factor — were rarely open to the Metis. In 1830, one-quarter of the labourers in the company were Metis; by 1850 over half the labourers were Metis. Even the mixed-blood children of company officers fared poorly in the company. The rank of apprentice postmaster was created for these children, Europeans started at the higher rank of apprentice clerk.

The Metis fared no better under the NWC. There too, they often worked in the lower-rank positions. However, there appeared to be a wider array of jobs available, including that of voyageur (not as romantic as it sounds — these were the people who transported the goods), guide, interpreter, hunter, cook, and mail transporter. Occasionally a Metis would rise to become a trader.

After the companies amalgamated, a number of employees were released. Many of those were Metis. Other Metis found the HBC too restrictive. As a result many Metis became independent traders, obtaining their goods and selling their furs in the United States. The HBC attempted to discourage this trade — much to the anger of the Metis.

The Metis' commitment to the principle of free trade in furs was encouraged by the arrival of Metis immigrants from the United States, where there was no trade monopoly. By the early 1800s there was a belt of over fifty mixed-blood settlements in the United States, stretching from the southern tip of Lake Michigan to the Red River. As the United States expanded westward these people had to make a choice: integrate into the American mainstream or move. Many (but not all) chose to leave and moved to the Red River area.

One of the best known American Metis settlements was Pembina, referred to by some commentators as the first capital of the Metis, and believed to have been established in the 1780s. It was a thriving community with its own schools and churches and by far the biggest Metis settlement, with over five hundred people calling it home. Cuthbert Grant was one of its leading citizens and he was responsible for its end as an important Metis town. An 1823 international survey put Pembina on the American side of the border. The British colonial authorities and the HBC, fearing that the Pembina Metis would fall under American influence and become trade competitors, worked through Grant to convince the people of Pembina to move north. In return for agreeing to move, they were given land in the parish of St. Boniface on the east side of the Red River, opposite its junction with the Assiniboine River, and in the White Horse Plains region west of the Assiniboine.

The influx of these Metis only gave more encouragement to the notion of free trade in furs, but the company fought back to preserve its monopoly. In the 1820s the HBC passed stringent regulations which, among other things, prohibited natives from trading or selling furs amongst themselves, made illegal the use of furs as gifts and gave HBC employees the power to search residences without search warrants to see if furs were being kept for private use. Any furs found were seized without compensation.

By 1845 Metis leaders were publicly asking the company to relax its strict trading policies. The Metis engaged Alexander Isbister, a mixed-blood born in Cumberland House (today, in northeastern Saskatchewan) and educated in Scotland, to present their case in London. He argued in front of the secretary of the colonies, backed by a petition with 977 names from the Red River area, that free trade was necessary if native people were to develop into worthy citizens. He accused the company of keeping natives "in a state of utter dependence." The company responded that it had been granted the sole legal right to trade in the west and that the free traders were in fact breaking the law.

The Metis free traders were aided by the fact that there was a growing market for their furs across the American border. By 1844 Norman Kittson had set up a post at Pembina to buy furs from the Metis. In ten years Metis sales in the United States rose from $5,000 to well over $150,000.

The company decided to take legal proceedings against the Metis. This was a bold step for, while the company had a legal monopoly, the Metis were the most powerful military force in the west. Perhaps the company was somewhat heartened by the arrival of the 300 man 6th Foot Regiment of The Royal Warwickshires.

The most famous of the trials took place on May 17, 1849, when the company charged four Metis with contravening its monopoly. The first to be tried was Pierre-Guillaume Sayer. The morning before the trial some two hundred to three hundred Metis, organized into a self-defence league, gathered on the steps of the St. Boniface Cathedral, across the river from the courthouse, to listen to a speech on free trade by Louis Riel, father of the Louis Riel who would lead the 1869-70 Metis government. After lunch the crowd converged on the courthouse. They packed the courtroom, many of them carrying their hunting rifles, powder horns and shot pouches. A jury was chosen and the trial began. The evidence made it clear that Sayer had traded whisky for furs and broken the company's monopoly. The jury, after finding Sayer guilty, recommended mercy; the judge agreed (undoubtedly influenced by the presence of two hundred armed men) and Sayer was released with a warning, whereupon the company dropped the charges against Sayer's three companions. When Sayer emerged from the courthouse announcing that he had been set free, the crowd fired off their guns and roared, "Vive la liberté! La commerce est libre!"

Land, Racism and the Birth of Metis Nationalism

The HBC stimulated Metis nationalism in other ways as well. Take the company's land policies. While the HBC generously sold 116,000 acres to Lord Selkirk for ten shillings, it was not quite so generous with the Metis.

First, the company did not sell land to locals; the most it would do was lease it. Practically speaking, such leases were close to outright sales because they were for 999 years. Before a lease was granted, however, it had to be paid for in cash, a commodity in short supply in the west because the only commercial enterprise was the HBC. And the company did little to increase the money supply since, rather than pay cash for furs, services and buffalo meat, it often paid by giving credit towards its goods.

There were other requirements to obtain land. One-tenth of the land had to be cultivated in short order, otherwise it reverted to the company. And before the land could be passed on or sold, the transfer had to be approved by the company.

Unable to meet these terms, the majority of the Metis simply ignored the HBC. As far as they were concerned the land was sitting unused, and so they simply took possession. When a father died he passed on the land to his sons. Whether a Metis was a hunter or trader, his land served as a home.

In addition to being denied legal title to their land, the Metis found themselves excluded from the Red River society. While the company had always discriminated against native people, in the 1840s and 1850s racism became more pronounced. By this time, a number of Europeans were living in the west, particularly in the Red River area. Many were company people who had brought their European families with them. As white settlement started to develop so did the notion — rooted in the social Darwinism of the age — that some people were superior to others. Whites came to be seen as the embodiments of civilization; the Metis, in contrast, were regarded as near savages fit only for menial employment.

By the 1850s the Metis were excluded from the social, economic and political life of the developing western settlements. Lelitia Hargrave, the wife of a prominent HBC official, wrote to a friend about a visitor she was expecting. The visitor had a Metis wife. "I hate the very thought of a half-breed visitor," Lelitia wrote. A bright Red River boy studying at the University of Toronto wrote agonizingly to his sister, "What if mama is an Indian!"

Over a hundred years later Howard Adams was still able to write in his book, *Prison of Grass*: "These half-breed people did not have a choice as to whether they would be Indians or whites or in-between; society defined them as members of the native society and it still does today."

Agriculture Comes West

In the 1850s the residents of Canada West (later the province of Ontario), dazzled by the agricultural potential of the western plains, began to argue against the continuation of the region's status as a fur-trade preserve. In 1857 a select House of Commons committee in London held hearings into the land administered by the HBC. The company's Governor, Sir George Simpson, testified, "I do not think that any part of the Hudson's Bay Company's Territories is well adapted for settlement; the crops are very uncertain." He was contradicted by Alexander Isbister, the Metis agent in London, who accused the company of hindering development in the west and keeping the inhabitants backward and ignorant.

Two expeditions were sent out. Captain John Palliser, who travelled into southwestern Saskatchewan and southeastern Alberta, reported that he found an extension of the American desert. An expedition led by Simon Dawson and Henry Hind travelled into the prairie parkland and found a rich fertile belt. Farther east, Canadian visionaries were talking of a dominion stretching from sea to sea, with the prairies to be the future dominion's bread-basket. These political pressures, coupled with the fact that furs were now becoming more scarce, made the HBC's monopoly less valuable. So the company, under pressure from the British government, began to think about selling their land to the government of Canada.

By this time the Metis were boiling over and ready for their biggest fight to date. They resented the decades of restrictions that the Company had placed on their lives and their exclusion from the management of the HBC and western society as a whole. They knew about organizing. For decades they had organized massive buffalo hunting expeditions involving hundreds of men. As a result of the buffalo hunt they fought (and won) battles against Indian tribes for buffalo grounds. They had fought to block the Selkirk colony (and lost) and successfully fought the HBC on the free trade issue. Now they were desperate, because with the decline of the buffalo and with settlement encroaching, they were fighting for a way of life. The stage was set for the rise of Louis Riel and the events of 1869-70.

3

The Government of Manitoba

Two provincial capitals have statues of Riel — Winnipeg and Regina. Regina's is symbolic of Canadians' curiosity about the man. In the dark of night, more than one teenager and adult has crept up to it to verify whether there is truth to the rumour that Riel's genitals remain uncovered under the cloak.

Few Canadian historical figures have been the source of as much debate and curiosity as Riel. In books, articles and speeches he has been described as everything from "an unrecognized father of Confederation" and Canada's "first human rights advocate" to an "inveterate masturbator" (by the psychiatrist who testified in his defence). Until the 1960s, Riel was classified by most Canadians as a murderer and a traitor. Then, as Canadian guilt over treatment of its native citizens grew, Riel became a hero. Today, there is a movement to have him pardoned posthumously.

Unfortunately, this preoccupation with Riel has caused Canadians to overlook the fact that the events of 1869 and 1885 were primarily caused not by Riel, but by deep-seated social and political problems. This is not to detract from Riel; he played an important role in the Metis' fight for justice. However, history is clear that, with or without Riel, the events of 1869 and 1885 would have occurred.

The Making of a Hero

That Louis David Riel became interested in Metis politics is hardly surprising. As already recounted, twenty years prior to the events in the Red River, in 1849, Louis Riel Sr. was one of the leaders of the free-trade movement in the Red River area.

Riel Sr. was a successful miller. His ethnic origin was primarily French, though his mother was believed to be of mixed French and Chipewyan origin. He married Julie Lagimodière, daughter of the first white woman to settle in the west, in 1843. A year later the first of their eleven children, Louis, was born.

Coming from the privileged merchant class, young Riel was able to indulge in the luxury of school. His success at his studies attracted the attention of the local bishop, who was always on the lookout for bright young boys for the priesthood. As a result, in 1858 Louis was sent to the Sulpician College in Montreal. He spent nearly ten years there studying law, humanities and classics. During his stay in Montreal he also took up employment in a law office, which led to an acquaintance with many of French Canada's leading political figures, including young Wilfrid Laurier. He also fell madly in love with a charming young French woman and proposed marriage to her. But it was not to be; her parents rejected Riel because of his Metis background, even though in blood he was mostly French. According to several historians, this event was a crucial step in Riel's politicization.

Riel's failure in love led to his dropping his studies and wandering first to Chicago and then to Minneapolis and eventually back to the Red River. He returned home at a critical time in the history of the west.

In the 1860s the Red River area was a hotbed of tension. Crop failures left many farmers destitute, and the vanishing buffalo and declining fur trade threatened the way of life of those Metis who survived by hunting and trapping. At the same time, the settlers who were pouring in represented a threat not only to established farmers but also to the Metis and Indians. All three groups feared that the newcomers would be a severe drain on the region's limited resources.

Racism was rampant. The English-speaking Half-breeds, looked down upon by English Protestants, were finding it equally difficult to gain acceptance among their French Catholic counterparts. The French-speaking Metis fared no better; the English Protestants who were starting to dominate the colony scorned the Metis because they had Indian and French blood, and were Catholic. Land-hungry Protestant fanatics led by Dr. John Christian Schultz tried to grab up as much land as possible, partly to make money and partly to prevent the colony from being overrun by French colonists.

To further complicate matters, Americans in Minnesota were advocating that the Red River be annexed to the United States. And if push came to shove, there was no one strong enough to resist the Americans. The HBC had largely lost its authority over the area. Its licence to trade in British Columbia and in the North-West (those lands in Canada's north, northern Alberta, and north-western Saskatchewan from which the waters flow into the Arctic

Ocean) expired in 1859 (though the company continued to trade in those areas). It retained the right to trade in Rupert's Land (essentially those lands from which the water drained into Hudson's Bay, and including most of the Canadian prairies); however, its ability to enforce its authority over that area was in some question after the English withdrew their troops from the area in 1861. And with the fur trade in rapid decline the company was too busy trying to consolidate its operations to provide effective management over the region.

There were three alternatives for the west: become a British colony, become a part of the United States, or become a part of the newly formed Dominion of Canada.

The answer came from Ottawa, there was no consultation with the local Metis, Indian or white residents. At the time of Confederation, the drafters of the British North America Act had made specific provision for the west to become a part of Canada. On December 16 and 17, 1867, Parliament in Ottawa adopted a resolution asking Her Majesty "to unite Rupert's Land and the North-Western Territory with this Dominion...." The resolution was introduced by William McDougall, Minister of Public Works, who was later appointed as the first lieutenant-governor of the North-West. Early in 1869 the British Parliament passed legislation authorizing the HBC to sell its land to the Canadian government. McDougall was one of the Canadian negotiators, and after some arm twisting by the British colonial secretary, a deal was reached in late March. Canada agreed to pay the Company 300,000 British pounds, to allow the company to retain 50,000 acres around its trading posts and to allow it to have almost two square miles in every township (a unit of land-measurement in western Canada equalling thirty-six square miles). The transfer date was set for December 1, 1869.

As part of the transfer the Canadian government agreed to fulfil certain conditions concerning Indian people. In the case of the Northwest Territory, the condition was that "...the claims of the Indian tribes to compensation for lands required for the purposes of settlement will be considered and settled in conformity with the equitable principles which have uniformly governed the British Crown in its dealings with the aborigines." The conditions attached to the transfer of Rupert's Land were that "...it will be the duty of the Government to make adequate provision for the protection of the Indian tribes whose interests and well-being are involved in the transfer." There was a further condition that "any claims of Indians to compensation for lands required for purposes of settlement shall be disposed of by the Canadian Government in communication with the Imperial Government; and the Company shall be relieved of all responsibility in respect of them." Today, four central Alberta Indian bands are suing the federal government on the grounds that it has not lived up to these conditions.

The deal made no mention of Metis claims. Was this an oversight or was it deliberate?

One legal scholar, Kent McNeil, in *Native Claims in Rupert's Land and the North-Western Territory: Canada's Constitutional Obligations*, argues that the wording in the conditions of transfer is wide enough to cover the Metis. He contends that the word Indian as used in the conditions of transfer includes all people with

Indian blood. As well, there is evidence to indicate that in the mid-1800s colonial and federal official did not distinguish between the Indians and Metis. For example, in the 1870s the Metis were allowed to join Indian tribes in signing treaties.

McNeil's interpretation is not universally accepted. In 1939, Canada's Supreme Court had to rule on the meaning of the word "Indians" in the Constitution, under which the federal government has financial responsibility for "Indians and Lands Reserved for Indians." At the heart of the 1939 dispute between Quebec and Ottawa was responsibility for programmes for the Inuit in northern Quebec. In making its decision the court chose to look at what the word "Indian" meant in 1867 and turned to a census conducted by HBC in the 1850s for clarification because, in the words of one judge, the HBC "possessed considerable powers of government and administration." In that census the Inuit were listed as Indians; but the "half-breeds" were not. They were listed with the whites. On that basis, the court concluded that Inuit were "Indians" and therefore a federal responsibility. If the census alone were the deciding factor in interpreting the word "Indian" in the Northwest Territory and Rupert's Land transfer agreements it is clear the federal government assumed no responsibility to settle with the Metis.

Whether or not the transfer agreements covered the Metis, one thing is certain: the Metis themselves felt ignored, even betrayed in the deal — and they reacted accordingly.

In the fall of 1869, in anticipation of acquiring control over the HBC territories, the government of Canada sent out survey parties to the Red River area. One of these parties, headed by Colonel John Dennis, set foot on André Nault's land on October 11. Nault, a cousin of Riel, went to speak to the surveyors; however, he spoke no English and the surveyors spoke no French. He left to find some help and an hour later he returned with 18 men. The only one who spoke English was twenty-five-year-old Louis Riel. He told the surveyors to leave and they did. But matters did not rest there.

Flushed with their initial success, the Metis decided to take additional action. They formed a national committee, of which Riel was elected secretary, and mounted a guard at the U.S. border to prevent William McDougall, the lieutenant-governor designate, from entering the territory. McDougall returned to Pembina, North Dakota, on November 2 to await the official transfer date of the territory.

One of the funniest incidents involved with the transfer had McDougall sneaking across the American border into Manitoba in the early hours of December 1 and reading a proclamation asserting his authority as governor. Apparently only the wind and stars heard him, though he did find a pole to nail the proclamation to. He then snuck back across the border. Ironically, without his knowledge Ottawa and London had postponed the transfer date — not only did he read his proclamation to the wilderness but it was of no legal effect.

On November 2 the Metis seized Upper Fort Garry, the strongest military bastion in the area, without firing a shot. The fort's occupants moved to Lower Fort Garry, but were forced to surrender on December 7 when their winter's supply of food (mostly pork) was captured by the Metis. The pork had been stored in the house of Dr.

Schultz, one of the white settlers who supported federation with Canada. When Schultz's house was seized some fifty Canadians, including Schultz, Captain Charles Boulton and Thomas Scott, were arrested. The next day the Metis established a government with John Bruce as its first president. Several weeks later Bruce was succeeded by Riel.

One of the government's earliest problems was deciding what to do with Boulton, Schultz and Scott. Boulton was sentenced to death, but his sentence was commuted. He would go on to fight the Metis at Batoche fifteen years later. Schultz managed to escape and headed for Ontario to lead a crusade to save the west from the French Catholic Metis.

Thomas Scott proved to be Riel's downfall. After his arrest Scott managed to escape twice but was recaptured each time. He was a bit of a thug: earlier in 1869, while working on a road gang between Lake of the Woods and Fort Garry, he was convicted of assault on the government official supervising the construction. His contempt for the Metis almost led to his being shot on more than one occasion. The government charged him with a number of offences, including assaulting a guard, plotting violence against the government and advocating overthrow of the government. A seven-man court martial convened by Ambroise Lepine, a Metis military commander, found Scott guilty and sentenced him to death. He was executed by firing squad on March 4, 1870.

Scott's death made him a martyr in the minds of many people in Ontario, and the same people used his execution to support their claim that Riel was a murderer. But legally, Riel had little to do with Scott's death. He did not sit on the panel of judges which sentenced Scott, nor was he part of the firing squad which carried out the sentence. And while he testified at Scott's court martial, according to several historical reports he also "pleaded that leniency be shown to the accused."

Of course, the Riel government did more than just deal with its opponents. Its December 8, 1869 declaration made clear that it wanted to establish relations with Canada. The document stated that the government "would enter into such negotiations with the Canadian government as may be favorable for the good government and prosperity of this people." At the same time, there is evidence which indicates that Riel and the Metis specifically rejected American overtures to join the United States.

Not all Metis were in favour of the government. In particular, support among the English speaking Half-Breeds wavered. On the other hand, some non-Metis were supportive and saw the government as a means of protesting the way in which their concerns had been ignored in the transfer of the former HBC territory to the Dominion of Canada.

The Case for the Metis Government

Riel's legal training served him well in defending his government. Riel claimed that all the HBC had was an exclusive right to trade in the west — it did not own the land or the people. All Canada bought was the trade monopoly. His position has legal merit in that the conditions of transfer required that Canada settle Indian land claims. If, in fact, the HBC owned the land outright, there would be no need for Canada to settle Indian claims. Obviously the negotiators realized that the Company's interest was a limited one.

Riel argued that the Metis had the right to determine if they would join Canada, and on what terms. He claimed that, since the Canadian government had not consulted the residents of the North-West with respect to the transfer it had violated the "rights of man" and the Metis were justified under the "law of nations" in forming their own government. Riel's argument is convincing and presages the international standard established 100 years later in the International Covenant on Civil and Political Rights. This document, which has been accepted by over 80 nations, stipulates that all peoples have the right to determine whether they will be incorporated into a nation state, and if so, on what basis.

According to Riel's argument, the Metis government and Canada were two sovereign nations. They entered into an international treaty whereby the Metis agreed to join Canada. If the treaty was breached then the other party would have the option to withdraw.

For Riel, even if the HBC was representative of the people, it had abandoned its role as the government of the west. As the Canadian government did not take immediate control, Riel argued that there was no effective government, and so the people were justified in establishing a government of their own. The facts would seem to be on his side. The transfer date was initially set as December 1, 1869. However, in view of the political difficulties, that takeover was delayed until July 15, 1870. Because the Metis government was the only government in the area from December 1869 to July 1870, it was entitled to enforce law and order during that period. Under this authority it had the right to arrest, try and punish Scott. Further, the common penalty for treason at the time was the death sentence.

Opponents of this argument suggest that there was no authority in the region because the Metis blocked the Canadian government from asserting its jurisdiction. While there is some merit to this argument, there is also another side. Technically, the HBC was the legal government until the date of the transfer. However, reality was different. Once it became clear to the company that it was going to have to give up some of its power in the North-West it did little to maintain its governing role. The company's raison d'être, after all, was to make money and there was little profit in fulfilling a governing role which it had agreed to give up in the near future. Further, after 1861, when the army was withdrawn, the company had no means of enforcing its authority. Therefore, prior to the transfer date (initially December 1, 1869 but post-poned until July 15, 1870) there was a government, the HBC, in name only.

Today, the Metis give new voice to Riel's arguments. For them, Riel was not a rebel but a legitimate head of government, and the events of 1869 were not a rebellion because there was no authority to rebel against. They also reject the term "provisional government" as a term used by contemporary non-Metis historians. For them the term "provisional" implies something intended to be tempo-rary. They argue that, had their negotiations to enter Confederation failed, their government might still be ruling today.

Demands of the Metis Government

History is rarely a set of indisputable facts. What were the final demands of the Metis government which formed the basis of its negotiation with Ottawa? It is generally agreed that two lists of the demands were drawn up — the first in December 1869 and the second in February 1870. Gerald Friesen in *The Canadian Prairies* suggests that the second list was amended by Riel, unbeknownst to the convention of forty which had drawn it up. Friesen then suggests that the list was amended yet again at the insistence of Bishop Taché, the Catholic bishop at St. Boniface who served as one of the advisers to the Metis. Father Ritchot, who would later be one of the three delegates who took the list to Ottawa, is also believed to have been involved in drafting the list. The clergy was actively involved in preparing the list as it wanted to ensure that the west remained French and Catholic.

As best as can be determined these were some of the principal demands:

- Provincehood for the west (to be called Assiniboia)
- Representation in the Senate and Commons
- Transfer payments from Ottawa
- That all males, including Indians, have the right to vote, except those Indian males living in unsettled areas
- That English and French be the official languages
- That the lieutenant-governor and the judges of the Supreme Court of the province be bilingual
- Public support for denominational schools (Friesen claims that this demand may have been added by

Bishop Taché)
- A senate for the province (at that time, upper chambers were a common feature in the provinces)
- That the Canadian government enter into treaties with all Indian tribes in Assiniboia, after consulting with the province
- A general amnesty covering all acts by all members of the Metis government

Three of the demands were of particular importance and are the source of debate today. They are reproduced here in their entirety:

5. That all properties, rights, and privileges enjoyed by the people of this Province, up to the date of our entering into Confederation, be respected, and that the arrangement and confirmation of all customs, usages, and privileges be left exclusively to the Local Legislature.

11. That the Local Legislature of the Province of Assiniboia shall have full control over all the public lands in the Province, and the right to amend all acts or arrangements made or entered into with reference to the public lands of Rupert's Land and the North West, now called the Province of Assiniboia.

19. That all debts contracted by the Provincial Government of the Territory of the North West, now called Assiniboia, in consequence of the illegal and inconsiderate measures adopted by Canadian officials to bring about the civil war in our midst, be paid out of the Dominion Treasurer; and that none of the members of the Provisional Government, or

> any of those acting under them, be in any way liable
> or responsible with regard to the movement or any
> of the actions which led to the present negotiations.

The list of demands did not specifically include land for
the Metis. Thomas Flanagan, a political scientist at the
University of Calgary and one of the strongest opponents
of the recognition of Metis rights, cites this fact as proof
that the Metis did not see themselves as having any
aboriginal rights. He says all they wanted was control of
the public lands. Joe and Patricia Sawchuk and Theresa
Ferguson argue in *Metis Land Rights in Alberta: A
Political History* that Riel saw clauses 5 and 11 as
guaranteeing Metis rights. He assumed that Manitoba
would continue to be a Metis province, and, by controlling public lands, would be able to compensate the Metis
for just claims. Until 1870 all provinces had control of
public lands. However, when Manitoba was created the
federal government retained control over public lands
and continued to do so until 1930.

Clause 19 was not only an amnesty clause, but also an
important acknowledgement of the federal government's
sole responsibility for the disastrous events of 1869-70.

The Province of Manitoba

Joseph Howe, then Minister of State for the Provinces,
wrote to William McDougall, lieutenant-governor designate, in December 1869, instructing him to assure residents of the North-West that all property rights enjoyed
under HBC rule would be recognized, that a most liberal
policy in granting title to occupied land would be fol-

lowed, and that all civil and religious liberties would be respected. In mid-January 1870 these commitments were reported in the press. As it turned out, they were not honoured.

Negotiations with Riel's government began in January 1870 when Ottawa sent three negotiators to Manitoba; the most prominent was Donald Smith, chief factor of the HBC in Canada, who had volunteered to act as mediator. On a cold frosty day at a meeting held outdoors because there was no building which could hold the crowd of two thousand people, Smith outlined the federal position. Interest was so high that the meeting continued the next day. Smith was not empowered to negotiate a settlement; his instructions were to use his influence to convince the Metis to lay down their arms.

The immediate result of Smith's address was the drawing up of a list of demands. After considerable discussion and amendment, not always agreed to by the whole community, the list was taken to Ottawa. Three delegates arrived in Ottawa early in April to negotiate the terms of entry into Confederation. To their surprise, the public was enraged over the hanging of Thomas Scott, and two of the delegates spent several days in jail.

One of the most important issues in the negotiations concerned land. Metis negotiators wanted control of public lands to be in the hands of the local legislature. Macdonald insisted that all public lands had to remain in federal control to ensure that the national dream, settlement of the west, could be carried out without local hindrance. According to one version of what happened next, Ritchot suggested, as a compromise, that the federal government retain control over public lands but that all settlers be guaranteed title to land they occupied and an additional reserve of land be set aside for the Metis. The government agreed and offered 100,000 acres to the Metis in addition to the land they already occupied. After further bargaining this was raised to 1.4 million acres — 140 acres for each Metis resident.

Ritchot demanded that the distribution of the Metis lands be in the hands of the Manitoba legislature. The government negotiators, John A. Macdonald and George-Étienne Cartier, insisted that they could never get such a provision through the House of Commons. Instead, they suggested that they would appoint individuals acceptable to Manitoba's Metis residents to supervise the distribution of land. This promise was never kept; control of land distribution remained in Ottawa and resulted in policies and practices which made it difficult, and in some cases impossible, for the Metis to get land.

Thomas Flanagan argues that the government had no intention of recognizing Metis rights in the Manitoba Act; its goal, he says, was only to buy out the Metis quickly and cheaply. He cites a speech John A. Macdonald delivered in the House of Commons on July 6, 1885. "In that Act [the Manitoba Act]," Macdonald said,

> ...it is provided that in order to secure the extinguishment of Indian title 1,400,000 acres of land should be settled upon the families of the half-breeds living within the limits of the then Province. Whether they had any right to those lands or not was not so much the question as it was a question of policy to make an arrangement with the inhabitants of the Prov-

> ince...1,400,000 acres would be quite sufficient for
> the purposes of compensating these men for what
> was called the extinguishment of Indian title. That
> phrase was an incorrect one, for the half-breeds did
> not allow themselves to be Indians.

The argument against Flanagan is that no matter what
Macdonald's intentions were, he did in fact recognize
Metis rights by the very act of entering into a land
settlement with them. In contract law, motive is seldom
relevant. The effect of a contract is determined by its
wording, not by the motives of the parties signing it.
Similarly, the effect of legislation (like the Manitoba Act)
is determined by its wording, not by the motives of the
legislators. Only if there is considerable confusion in the
wording will courts try to determine the effect by looking
to see what the government intended.

The result of the negotiations was the Manitoba Act,
passed by Parliament on May 12, 1870, to take effect on
July 15. While the Act met one of the Metis' major
demands — the creation of a separate province — it was
not all they had hoped for. The Manitoba that was created
was a mere one hundred square miles. The rest of the west
became the Northwest Territories and was to be governed
directly by Ottawa. Similarly, Manitoba did not get
control of public lands, including lands set aside as a
Metis reserve, until 1930. The amnesty which had been
demanded by the Metis and promised by Ottawa was not
included in the Manitoba Act — an omission that angered
Riel to the point that he considered resisting Ottawa until
the amnesty was legislated. However, with most of the
Metis anxious to get on with the buffalo hunt, Riel gave

in. As he was soon to learn, Ottawa had no intention of living up to its promise.

If the Manitoba Act represented a great political victory for the Metis, the government made a mockery of that victory by limiting the territory the Metis could rule and ensuring that they had no control over the most important resource of all, land.

Manitoba After 1870: What Happened?

That the federal government had no intention of treating its commitments to the Metis seriously was soon evident. Despite the fact that local residents in Manitoba accepted the terms of Confederation in a public vote, the federal government sent Colonel Wolseley and twelve hundred men to the Red River. The army arrived one week in advance of Lieutenant-Governor Adams Archibald, McDougall's successor. It met no resistance; Riel had fled temporarily to the United States, and his compatriots had vacated Fort Garry prior to Colonel Wolseley's arrival. In fact, Louis Riel had insisted that the Union Jack be flown on the fort's standard to greet the army.

Wolseley and his men did not show the same courtesy to the Metis — they embarked upon a campaign of violence. On the day of their arrival some soldiers recognized Elzéar Goulet, a member of the court martial which had found Scott guilty. He was chased by the soldiers and was stoned to death as he tried to swim across the river. Soon afterwards, André Nault, another member of the court martial, was bayonetted and left for dead.

The soldiers' actions set an unfortunate precedent for Metis-white relationships in the new province. Racism and violence against the Metis became everyday occurrences which, coupled with the inability to gain land and the need to move west to find vanishing buffalo, led to a massive westward migration of Metis. In 1870 the population of Manitoba was 12,000, 10,000 of whom were mixed-blood people. Of the 10,000, 6,000 were Metis and the balance were English-speaking Half-breeds. Fifteen years later less than 7 per cent of the population were of mixed-blood origin. With the exception of an English-speaking Half-breed, John Norquay, who became premier of Manitoba in 1878, the Metis people did not play a significant role in the political history of Manitoba. They became outcasts in the province which they helped create.

The most significant defeat for the Metis came with their inability to obtain the land they were promised and title to land they already occupied. The Manitoba Act had two important provisions dealing with land. Section 31 purported to buy out the Metis' aboriginal rights to land. The section deals with the Metis as a group and not as individuals. Relevant parts of it read:

> And whereas, it is expedient, towards the extinguishment of the Indian Title to the lands in the Province, to appropriate a portion of such ungranted lands, to the extent of one million four hundred thousand acres thereof, for the benefit of the families of the half-breed residents, it is hereby enacted that...the Lieutenant-Governor shall select such lots or tracts in such parts of the Province as he may deem expedient,

to the extent aforesaid, and divide the same among the children of the half-breed heads of families residing in the Province....

Section 32 of the Act dealt with people, both Metis and non-Metis, who were already occupying land (occupied land was primarily riverlots along the Red and Assiniboine Rivers). First, it confirmed that those people who had obtained title from the HBC would have their title confirmed by the government. Second, even if a person did not have title but occupied the land with the permission of the company, he had a right to title. Third, the section provided that even if an individual had occupied the land without permission but was in "peaceful possession" of a parcel of land, he would have the first right to claim title. This latter provision offered protection for some fifteen hundred Metis families. Finally, the section stated that the lieutenant-governor was to make a fair adjustment for the haylots, located behind the riverlots, which people were using.

The Macdonald government had some doubts about its authority to pass the Manitoba Act. It approached the Imperial Parliament for an amendment to the British North America Act. That amendment, The British North America Act 1871, approved Parliament's actions in creating Manitoba. But it went further and declared that "...it shall not be competent for the Parliament of Canada to alter the provisions of the last-mentioned Act of the said Parliament in so far as it relates to the Province of Manitoba...."

As we shall see, this is a key point in the Manitoba Metis' lawsuit currently before the courts. They allege that the federal government unilaterally changed section 31 and 32 of the Manitoba Act. Because of the above provision in the 1871 Act, they say, its actions were unconstitutional.

In the 1870s and 1880s the federal government passed numerous acts and orders-in-council attempting to clarify the meaning of sections 31 and 32 and putting into place the machinery for the distribution of the benefits. The legislation even had names; an 1873 Act was called "An Act to Remove Doubts as to the Construction of Section 31...." Unfortunately, when one studies this legislation it quickly becomes apparent that the federal government ended up making the land distribution scheme extremely difficult to administer.

Historians such as Douglas Sprague from the University of Manitoba argue that both the Macdonald and Mackenzie governments were engaged in a deliberate conspiracy to deny the Metis those rights which they had been guaranteed by the Manitoba Act. What lay behind this conspiracy? Racism. Since it was not believed that the Metis could be good farmers, the plan was to drive them out into marginal areas where they could live by hunting and fishing. Besides ensuring that the west would be settled by hard-working white farmers, this plan had the advantage of assuaging fears of another Metis rebellion. Obviously, if the Metis were widely dispersed, they would find it much more difficult to organize politically than if they were concentrated in one area.

Federal legislation was not the only impediment which developed in the efficient distribution of land benefits promised under the Manitoba Act. Speculators did a booming business in Metis lands — often committing outright fraud against the Metis with the knowledge of the government. The Metis allege that the provincial government actively aided this process. They point to provincial legislation passed in the 1870s and 1880s, supposedly intended to clear up uncertainty regarding land titles, which had the effect of legalizing many questionable actions.

Even assuming there was no conspiracy it is clear that the excessive complexity of the system ended up costing the Metis much of their land.

The first lieutenant-governor, Adams Archibald, devised a plan in late 1870 for the allocation of the 1.4 million acres to which the Metis were entitled. His idea was to allot 140 acres to each mixed-blood person, the land to be taken from ungranted land immediately behind the riverlots which the Metis already occupied. This would allow them to remain near their riverlots and parishes. As Archibald read the section, every Metis — man, woman and child — was entitled to land.

Archibald sent his proposal to Joseph Howe, then Minister of State for the Provinces, but was instructed that the federal cabinet did not like his idea and that he should leave the matter to the Dominion government "without volunteering any interference."

The first problem arose over whether section 31 benefits applied only to children or to children and adults. Initially, the federal government agreed with Archibald's interpretation that benefits applied to all; however, in 1873 it declared that only children could benefit. By cutting out the adults the number of potential claimants was reduced from ten thousand to six thousand. In 1874 the parents were put back in, but the legislation left some doubt as to whether they could get land — the government was given the discretion of granting scrip certificates worth $160 which could be used to purchase land. It is alleged that the government almost always granted money scrip instead of land.

Matters were further complicated by the slowness with which the process moved. In 1870 the government decided to enumerate the Metis. That census took place two years later. Then in 1875 commissioners were appointed to examine claims. It took seven years before the first grants were made under section 31. Unscrupulous speculators often took powers of attorney (a legal document authorizing someone to handle your affairs) from the Metis in advance of any benefits or title to land being issued. The power of attorney allowed the speculator to claim benefits on behalf of the Metis when land or money scrip was eventually granted. In return, little compensation was given to the Metis.

A debate ensued in Manitoba on the extent to which the Metis should be protected from speculators. In 1873 Manitoba passed The Half-breed Land Grant Protection Act, which stated that no agreement signed by a Metis transferring his land prior to his obtaining title was to be binding. This meant that the speculators who used the Metis' powers of attorney to collect land might be out of luck. Equally affected would be people who subsequently bought Metis land from the speculators. There was, however, some protection for the speculator because he could sue to reclaim his money — of course, it was a realistic remedy only if the individual sued had other financial resources against which the judgement could be collected.

Lieutenant-Governor Morris (Archibald's successor) wanted to disallow the legislation "because it was novel and retroactive;" the federal Deputy Minister of Justice agreed that it was repugnant but allowed it on the condition that it be amended. The federal government's concern was that thousands of contracts for the sale of land would be put in jeopardy.

The Manitoba legislature agreed and changed the law to provide that any agreement by a Metis to sell his land rights was binding unless he returned the money within three months of passage of the law. The effect of this law was to place the onus on the Metis individual to challenge a transaction and gave him or her a short three month period to do it. And it obviously would have no effect on agreements entered into after the three month period. The final result of this law was to make valid transactions by which speculators had obtained land, regardless of the irregularities under which it had been purchased.

Much of the land under section 31 was for the benefit of children. Manitoba statutes were changed on a number of occasions in order to allow Metis children to sell their land — this at a time when the law made clear that non-Metis children had no right to sell land.

In 1878 Manitoba passed legislation allowing Metis minors between eighteen and twenty-one to sell their land with parental consent. A year later the requirement for parental consent was dropped. Then in 1881 Manitoba legislation allowed Metis children of any age to sell their land without parental consent. Finally in 1885 the Manitoba Legislature made things clear once and for all. An Act relating to the Titles of Half-Breed Lands declared that:

NORTHERN LIGHTS COLLEGE CENTRE

> In all cases where lands...belonging to infant half-breeds...have been sold...and whether the same shall have been executed by the parent or guardian or next friend or prothonotary of the court in behalf of the said infant...such conveyance shall be, and shall always be deemed to have always...been sufficient to vest in the grantee or grantees...all the estate thereby purported to be granted....

The effect of this legislation was to make it impossible ever to question any land transfers from Metis children to speculators. If a child's interest in land was sold by a drunken father for one dollar, no questions could be asked. Gerald Friesen in *The Canadian Prairies* gives an example of the extent of shady practices. Joseph Carriére's children transferred their land to lawyer-politician A. W. Ross, who became a substantial landowner. The petition by Carriére to sell his children's land was signed at the home of Napoléon Bonneau, who worked for Ross, and was witnessed by another of Ross's employees, R.P. Wood, grandson of Manitoba's Chief Justice. The petition was then approved by Judge Wood. The Carriére family never even saw the land nor did they set the price — that was set by Bonneau.

By 1886 all of the 1.4 million acres had been granted. Less than 20 per cent of the eligible Metis beneficiaries actually owned the land they were entitled to.

Douglas Sprague, in his article "Government Lawlessness in the Administration of Manitoba Land Claims, 1870-1887," concludes:

...it is impossible to say whether the hundreds of persons who collected scrip at the Dominion Lands office in Winnipeg on grounds that they were the authorized agents of the rightful claimant did indeed have such authorization. (The Powers of Attorney were mysteriously burned in a mail fire in route to Ottawa.)

The Metis fared no better when it came to section 32 rights, which guaranteed them title to the riverlots they occupied. As with section 31 claims, Archibald proposed a simple way of dealing with section 32 claims. He suggested that all claimants be required to post notice of their claim and, if there was no opposition, the claimant be declared the registered owner. In the event of conflicting claims, he proposed the holding of an inquiry to determine the rightful owner. According to his plan, all claims could be dealt with in a maximum of two years.

Again the federal government refused to follow his suggestion and instead adopted a procedure which stretched out the process over fifteen years. Then in the 1880s the government moved to place a cutoff date on claims even though many had not been processed because of complications introduced by the government. First, a cutoff of May 1, 1882 was established but that was later extended to May 1, 1886. The Metis claim that this limitation was illegal: there was no limitation in the original Manitoba Act, and so by imposing one the government was changing the Act, something the British Parliament said it could not do.

In addition to the time limitation there were many other roadblocks placed in the way of people trying to get title to their riverlots.

Before recognizing any claims, the government decided to survey the land, and the surveyors it appointed had considerable power. An 1876 order-in-council required sufficient improvements before "peaceful possession," the proof of which was necessary to obtain title, would be recognized. Improvements were proved by a surveyor's certificate, with the surveyor being the sole judge as to whether the improvements were sufficient. The Metis claim that a surveyor would often declare land unoccupied because he did not think there was sufficient cultivation or an acceptable dwelling on the property. On other occasions only part of the land would be recognized as improved. Thus, some claimants received eighty acres, others forty and a great many no land at all. This was contrary to the Manitoba Act because all that the Act required was "peaceful possession."

Furthermore, the haylots behind the riverlots were put up for homesteading even before the survey was completed. More than one Metis found homesteaders on his hayland. Orders-in-council in 1874 made clear that the new settlers were not to be dispossessed but the Metis could be compensated by the issuance of scrip certificates.

Federal legislation in 1875 left considerable confusion as to a Metis' rights if he wanted to advance a grievance. That legislation gave the Minister of the Interior the power to appoint commissions to investigate cases where there were competing claims. The commission was empowered to advise the minister as to who should get title to the land. There was no right of a commission in those cases where a Metis alleged that the government was denying his rightful claim. This in spite of the fact that 1873 legislation guaranteed everyone the right to take their case to the claims court. The 1873 Act was repealed by the 1875 Act.

Other impediments were put in a claimant's way. In 1872 provincial legislation declared that riverpaths made excellent highways. As a result, the government was entitled to expropriate a strip 120 feet wide along the rivers. It so happened that these strips cut through the Metis riverlots. In Kildonan it is estimated that one-fourth of the farms were ruined because the diagonal cut of the highways left the farmer two triangular plots at either end of his farm. In some cases the road even ran through houses and barns.

A great deal of paperwork was required to deal with riverlot claims. Claims were first examined in Winnipeg; if they passed this first hurdle they were sent to the Department of the Interior in Ottawa. Once that department was satisfied of the validity of the claim the papers were passed to the Deputy Minister of Justice to ensure all legalities were complied with. If the Department of Justice felt there was insufficient evidence it refused to act on the file.

Robert Lang was in charge of the claim files. He selected those claims with the strongest likelihood of success (those that met the requirements of the law) and brought them to the attention of his Manitoba associates, A. Mathewman and A.G.B. Bannatyne. Mathewman and Bannatyne visited the claimant, informing him that his claim was weak but that if he provided extra information to their man in Ottawa the obstacles could be cleared. The price was half the claimant's land. After the scheme was discovered, Lang fled the country. Federal officials decided that they had no responsibility to extradite and prosecute Lang because his activities were directed against individuals and not against the government itself. It was up to the wronged individuals to sue Lang, the government declared.

An example of the effect of this manoeuvring on the part of the government could be found in the community of Rat River. Ninety-three claims to riverlots were filed. Eighty-four were rejected outright because the occupants had insufficient cultivated land and either no dwelling or an unacceptable one. Five claimants who had adequate houses and at least five cultivated acres received forty-acre grants; four claimants who had houses and at least ten cultivated acres received eighty-acre grants.

A Century Later

For the past one hundred years the Manitoba Metis have felt aggrieved over what happened to them in the late 19th century. Over the years they have held meetings to discuss their complaints, they have talked to governments, their organizations have carried out historical and legal research to document their claims, and they have published papers, articles and books outlining their grievances.

In the late 1970s they decided to take action to seek redress. In 1979 the Manitoba Metis Federation began negotiations with the provincial and federal governments to resolve their longstanding grievances. After two years of no progress, the Federation launched a court action but abandoned it in the early 1980s in the hope of achieving a settlement with the newly elected NDP government. When negotiations again failed, the Metis resumed court action in 1986. In its case the Manitoba Metis Federation, joined by its Alberta counterpart and the Native Council of Canada, is asking for a declaration in the Court of Queen's Bench that some twenty-six federal and provincial statutes and orders-in-council passed between 1871 and 1886 were unconstitutional because they had the effect of changing the rights guaranteed under the Manitoba Act. They argue that the British North America Act of 1871 explicitly forbade the Canadian government from fundamentally changing the Manitoba Act. Details of the Metis allegations are spelled out in two statements of claim totalling thirty-five pages.

This is not the only Metis legal action currently underway in Manitoba. In a second lawsuit, this one in federal court, the Manitoba Metis are seeking damages (in land and money) from the federal government for breach of trust. The Metis contend that the federal government had an obligation in 1870 and continues to have an obligation to see that their interests are protected. They base their argument on a 1985 Supreme Court of Canada decision declaring that the federal government, when administering Indian lands, has a duty to obtain the best financial arrangement on behalf of Indian people. In short, the Supreme Court placed the federal government in the role of guardian of Indian lands. The Metis claim that the federal government has a similar duty to them and that the duty was breached when federal legislation deprived them of land they were entitled to. This lawsuit is on hold until such time as there is a final decision in the first suit.

In order to succeed in the second suit, the Metis will need an order (which is what the first suit is about) stating that the federal government acted illegally. Canada's court structure is such that two lawsuits are necessary. The federal government can be sued for damages only in the Federal Court — that court, however, cannot rule on the constitutionality of provincial legislation.

The first lawsuit became embroiled in procedural wrangling when, on January 7, 1987, federal lawyers asked Judge Gordon Barkman of the Manitoba Court of Queen's Bench to dismiss the Metis suit without hearing its merits (the Manitoba government decided not to fight on the procedural point). The federal government insisted that there was nothing to sue about. Their lawyers argued that the land promised under the Manitoba Act had in fact been distributed. Under the distribution scheme, title was given to individuals, and if there were irregularities in the distribution, only those individuals who had been wronged could sue. They also argued that the people who could claim benefits are now dead and that the plaintiff, the Manitoba Metis Federation, was not representative of the Metis who may have been deprived of land in the 1870s. Even if it was, they said, 117 years was too late to seek redress for a wrongdoing. The federal government further pointed out that, under Canada's constitution, responsibility for legislating over property rights rests with the provinces. Therefore, the federal government could not be responsible for statutes passed by the Manitoba government which may have had the effect of making it more difficult for the Metis to hold their land. Finally, the federal government suggested that the political forum was a more appropriate place for settling the dispute. Federal lawyer Ivan Whitehall told the court that the litigation was a sideshow and stated, "the main show is around the negotiating table." After the hearing, Manitoba Metis lawyer Yvon Dumont challenged Whitehall's statement, noting, "the government refuses to come to the table."

The Metis achieved their first small victory when the Court of Queen's Bench struck down the federal government's preliminary objections and decided that the matter should go to trial. The federal government appealed the judgement to the Manitoba Court of Appeal, which heard the case in mid-September 1987, and reserved judgement. At the time of writing it had not rendered its decision. No matter which side wins the procedural point at the Appeal Court, the decision will probably be appealed to the Supreme Court of Canada.

If the procedural point is resolved in favour of the Metis and the matter goes to trial, the case will be part of the Canadian legal scene for years to come. To start with, it will involve a detailed examination of more than 35 pieces of legislation and more than 1,100 government documents. Historians and political scientists — Thomas Flanagan is expected to testify on behalf of the government, and Douglas Sprague on behalf of the Metis — will be called to help interpret events and documents.

Representing the Manitoba Metis Federation is one of Canada's most prominent native rights advocates, Thomas Berger. Interest in the case is intense. If it goes ahead, it will not only re-examine the events that led to the formation of Manitoba but also review how some wealthy people in Manitoba built their fortunes. Today, much of the city of Winnipeg and its neighbouring suburbs sit on what the Metis allege was land set aside for them under the 1870 Manitoba Act.

Never before have the Metis, or for that matter anyone else, sued to assert their rights on this scale. The case promises to raise several fundamental questions. Did Prime Ministers John A. Macdonald and Alexander Mackenzie conspire against the Metis, or was it an accident of history that so few Metis ended up with land promised under the Manitoba Act of 1870? Did federal and provincial legislation racially discriminate against the Metis? Were the Metis too anxious to sell their rights for a quick dollar and thus the authors of their own misfortune, as Flanagan claims? Did the Metis abandon their land claims because they did not want to be part of a settled society?

In order to succeed the Metis will have to convince the courts that the Manitoba Act intended to confer benefits on the Metis as a group and not as individuals. Otherwise, only the individuals, all dead by now, could sue. They will also have to prove that federal and provincial legislation was specifically passed to deny the Metis, as a group, their land rights. The burden of proving the allegations rests with the Metis. While many government documents are available, there are no witnesses who can testify about their own experience and this may prove to be a handicap to the Metis. Sadly, the Metis could lose, not on substance, but on procedure.

The case has important ramifications for Metis everywhere. It is estimated that in western and northern Canada between 60 and 75 per cent of Metis can trace their origins to the Red River area. Presumably, all of these Metis could share in the fruits of a victory in Manitoba. Such a victory would also cast doubts on subsequent government-Metis dealings in other parts of western Canada. Above all, it would place pressure on governments to negotiate with Metis groups outside Manitoba in order to avoid other litigation.

In their statement of claim the Metis summed their goal up this way:

> The achievement of a land base for the Metis is the goal of the Manitoba Metis Federation...In pursuit of this goal, it would be greatly to the advantage of the Metis, in seeking agreement of the Government of Canada and the Government of Manitoba to enter into land claims negotiations, to obtain a declaration that the federal and provincial statutes and orders-in-council referred to...were unconstitutional measures....

A land base (a geographic area the Metis can call their own) is essential if the Metis are to become self-governing. It is difficult to imagine a government without an area of land over which it can rule.

Even if the Metis lose the lawsuit their grievances will not go away. They will look to other arenas to press their case. At most, a court can rule, based on evidence presented by the Metis, on whether the government acted illegally. A court ruling against the Metis would mean that the government acted within the letter of the law, but it would not mean that the Metis were fairly and justly treated. Legality and justice are not the same thing.

4

The North-West Rebellion

Since 1885, historians and political scientists have debated the causes of the North-West Rebellion, and in recent years the debate has heated up between those who claim it was the government's fault and those who blame the Metis and their leader, Riel. The only thing everyone can agree on is that the rebellion, by providing the incentive for pushing ahead with construction of the Canadian Pacific Railway, played an important role in the building of Canada. As well, for those who believe that nations are born under fire, the 1885 rebellion was the new dominion's first military adventure, and it ended in victory. However, there are other perspectives. The rebellion may have turned Canada into a country stretching from sea to sea, but, at the same time, Riel's execution on a charge of treason set English and French Canadians at each other's throats. All in all, the results of the rebellion — for white Canadians — were mixed.

For the losers in the rebellion, the Metis and the Indians, the costs of defeat were great. Many of the demands the Metis are advancing today are rooted in the events leading up to the rebellion, the rebellion itself, and its aftermath.

The Metis of the North-West

In the 1870s, according to conservative estimates, some 20,000 people lived in what was then the Northwest Territories (which included all of the west except British Columbia and the 100-square-mile Manitoba). Those 20,000 included 13,000 Indians, 5,000 Metis and 2,000 Europeans.

The Metis were primarily concentrated in three regions: the Cypress Hills (southwestern Saskatchewan), Central Alberta (primarily at Edmonton, St. Albert, Lac Ste. Anne and Lac La Biche) and the Batoche-St. Laurent area. Some three hundred Metis lived in the latter region in 1870. Between 1877 and 1883 the population of the Batoche-St. Laurent area was swelled by 1,450 Metis migrants from Manitoba. They not only moved to existing towns but formed new ones such as nearby St. Louis, and their arrival helped give the area the largest Metis population outside of Manitoba.

The migrants moved for many reasons. Those who lived by hunting buffalo moved west in the hopes of finding larger herds. Others left because of the growing racism in Manitoba. Still others left for cultural reasons; as English Protestant settlers poured into Manitoba, the Metis found that they were quickly becoming a minority. Finally, some left because of the legal and bureaucratic difficulties they were having in obtaining land.

They represented all classes. There were merchants like Xavier Letendre (nicknamed Batoche) who established a chain of trading posts headquartered in Batoche and built a house that rivalled the finest houses in Winnipeg. There were intellectuals like Charles Nolin who served as Minister of Agriculture in Manitoba and, of course, there were labourers, hunters and traders.

In the early 1870s the Metis in the Batoche area formed their own government with an elected council and president. In part, the council was filling the near-vacuum in government which existed in much of the west at the time. Nevertheless, the federal government had some fears of the council and ordered General Selby-Smith, head of the Canadian militia, to carry out an investigation. He reported, in 1875, that the council was essentially an extension of the organization set up to coordinate the buffalo hunt. Of course, one reason why the Metis banded together was to press the federal government to deal with their land claims.

The government's land policy for the North-West was first laid out in the Dominion Lands Act of 1872. Establishing a uniform policy for settlement in the west, the Act included a homesteads policy and a survey system whereby the land was divided into one-mile squares (called sections, with each section subdivided into four quarter sections and thirty-six sections making a township). Not all land was opened for homesteading. Land had been set aside for the HBC as part of the transfer agreement from the company to Canada, and some 25 million acres of land "fairly fit for settlement" was reserved for the CPR. Some land was reserved for sale. In a September 1882 petition, Gabriel Dumont and forty-six others put their marks to a petition complaining about having to pay two dollars an acre for land on odd-numbered sections which they had occupied before the survey.

Even prior to the establishment of a government in Batoche, petitions from the North-West Metis were sent to Ottawa demanding a land settlement similar to the one in Manitoba. Whether they were entitled to a land settlement in the 1870s remains an unanswered legal question. There were two grounds on which they based their claims: first, on the basis of aboriginal rights, and second, on the basis that the government had made a legally binding commitment to the Metis in Manitoba and justice demanded similar treatment for other Metis. The argument in favour of aboriginal rights rested on the Metis' Indian origins. Since the aboriginal rights of Indians had been recognized by the federal government when it entered into treaty negotiations, the Metis felt that they were entitled to the same consideration.

As the Metis population in the west increased, so too did their lobbying. Their efforts were aided by the Catholic clergy — in particular Father André of St. Laurent and Archbishop Taché, from St. Boniface, both of whom urged the government to deal fairly with the Metis. In 1879 the Macdonald government responded to the pressure. An amendment to the Dominion Lands Act gave cabinet the power:

> To satisfy any claims existing in connection with the extinguishment of the Indian title preferred by half-breeds resident in the North-West Territories outside the limits of Manitoba, on the fifteenth day of July, one thousand eight hundred and seventy, by granting

land to such persons, to such extent and on such terms
and conditions, as may be deemed expedient.

This provision applied only to those Metis who were
living in the North-West on July 15, 1870 (the day
Canada took over administration of the west from the
HBC), it did not cover the Metis who migrated from
Manitoba after 1870. The wording was amended in 1883
to make doubly clear that Manitoba migrants did not
qualify. Nor did this provision set aside land for the Metis.
It simply gave the federal cabinet the power, on such
terms as it saw fit, to reach settlements with them.

No action was taken to address Metis land claims until
January 1885, when an order-in-council was passed authorizing the creation of a commission to enumerate
those Metis who might be entitled to claim benefits.
Historians are divided as to what this order-in-council
actually meant; Ken Hatt claims that it referred only to
those Metis resident in the North-West in 1870, while
Thomas Flanagan sees it as applying to all Metis. What-
ever the case, the commission did not begin its work until
after the rebellion had started, and by that time it did have
the power to deal with all Metis. The government's
explanation for the six-year delay between the time
legislation was passed and action taken was that it was
trying to determine the best way to settle with the Metis
and avoid the problems which had arisen in Manitoba.

The Survey System, Homesteading Regulations and Speculators

After the establishment of the grid survey system by the

Dominion Lands Act of 1872, survey teams were sent to establish meridians or base lines running on a north-south axis across western Canada. The need to do such preliminary work, coupled with the size of the west, meant that many areas were not surveyed until the late 1870s and 1880s. By the time the survey reached the Batoche area, in 1878, many Metis had staked out riverlots for their use, just as they had done in the Red River area and their French forefathers had done in Quebec. The average riverlot, containing approximately 200 acres, did not conform to the survey system of one-mile squares (sections), each subdivided into four quarter sections of 160 acres.

While official policy stated that the survey was to accommodate riverlots wherever found, what actually happened did not always conform with policy. In the Batoche area only 20 per cent of the land was surveyed into riverlots. The balance was surveyed into sections and quarter-sections. The decision not to divide all the land into riverlots was made by the two surveyors assigned to the area. Not finding many people, and unable to speak the language of those they did meet, they decided that there was no need to extend the riverlot survey system.

When the Metis protested, the government refused to resurvey the land, trying rather to fit the Metis riverlots into the quarter-sections already surveyed. Each quarter-section was further subdivided into four legal subdivisions of forty acres. Using such forty-acre parcels, the government tried to give a Metis title to his riverlot by granting five forty-acre plots, but this proved bureaucratically complex and rarely did five legal subdivisions match the shape of a riverlot. The pointlessness of it all was recognized after the rebellion, in 1889-90, when all of the area was resurveyed into riverlots.

There were other difficulties with the survey. An official survey plan of the riverlots was not published until 1884. Normally, such plans were published within a year of the survey. Until a survey plan was published the occupants of such lots could not get a government-recognized title to their land from the Dominion land titles office, and without title they could not legally deal with their property. The delay raised Metis suspicions that they would be driven off the land.

The very fact of the survey heightened Metis suspicions. Those who had migrated from Manitoba were well aware of the powers that surveyors had — some undoubtedly recalled that it was the surveyor who decided if an occupant was in "peaceful possession" of a riverlot. Surveyors entered onto the land without permission of the occupants. Few surveyors spoke French or Cree and many Metis spoke no English.

Matters were further complicated by the federal government's homesteading policy, which entitled a person to file a claim to a 160-acre homestead upon payment of a ten dollar fee. After a three-year period of occupancy and sufficient improvements, title to the land went to the homesteader. The federal government's position was that Metis who occupied land after the homesteading policy was announced had to comply with homestead regulations. What this meant was that some of the Metis arriving from Manitoba had yet another set of bureaucratic hurdles to face.

Few Metis appear to have been deprived of land as a result of the government's survey and homesteading policy. William Pearce, the government's chief surveyor, wrote after the rebellion that "the river lot question had no more to do with the outbreak than the change of the moon." (His comments were discredited by many local reports which indicated that Pearce did not speak French or Cree and made no attempt to communicate with local people when he visited the area). Nevertheless, it is clear that issues relating to the survey created distrust and uncertainty, and added to the tensions brewing in the west.

Compounding the Metis' frustrations were the activities of land speculators. In the 1870s, in anticipation of the transcontinental railway, speculators began to acquire large blocks of land in western Canada. Federal land policy, as expressed in the Dominion Lands Act, was amended in 1874 to allow such acquisitions. The government's hope was that, by giving large blocks of land to so-called colonization companies, it would be relieved of some of its responsibility in settling the west.

The original plan called for the CPR line to be built through the prairie parkland, touching near points such as Prince Albert, Battleford and Edmonton. The Prince Albert Colonization Land Company obtained substantial parcels of land south of Prince Albert in the belief that the railway would pass there. The company had good political connections, with twenty-four Conservative members of Parliament and senators serving on its board of directors. Surveyors were given shares for assisting the company. Some of the land which the company claimed was land on which Metis lived. Both Howard Adams and

Don McLean, author of *1885: Metis Rebellion or Government Conspiracy?*, maintain that when there was a conflict between the company and a Metis occupant over title, government surveyors and land-title officials always sided with the company.

The company was not alone in grabbing land around Prince Albert. The area was full of speculators who had visions of achieving great wealth when the railway came west. Much of the land on which they saw their wealth being built was land occupied by the Metis.

One successful speculator was Lawrence Clarke, who presented himself as a friend of the Metis and who ended up playing a crucial role in the 1885 rebellion. Clarke, the HBC factor at Fort Carlton (located between Saskatoon and Prince Albert), was born into wealth in Ireland and received a good education before coming to work for the company. As Carlton was a major HBC distribution point, serving much of the northern and central prairies, there was a need for freighters (people who could transport goods and furs great distances) and other labourers. Clarke played an important role in the founding of the Metis colony of St.Laurent-Batoche by encouraging the Metis to settle there, reasoning that a nearby Metis settlement would be a good source of cheap labour for the company. He was elected chairman of the first Batoche-St. Laurent council in the early 1870s.

Clarke wanted to become rich and famous; the first goal he satisfied through land speculation and the second through politics (he was elected to the North-West Council in 1881). He also enjoyed the exercise of power. While on the one hand he supported the Metis, he often used them as a tool to further his own interests. According to

Adams and McLean, Clarke ended up working for the federal government as an agent whose job was to provoke a rebellion.

Indians and Whites

Metis discontent, stemming from conflicts with speculators and the federal survey and homestead policy, has to be seen in the context of the general level of frustration in the west. Both the Indians and many white farmers were frustrated by policies of the faraway federal government, which ruled the west as a colony.

The Indian people found themselves in a desperate situation. Smallpox was rampant on the prairies and at the same time the buffalo were vanishing. Treaties had been signed and Indians were confined to reserves, where conditions were even worse than the devastation that had faced them before confinement. When the government, in a cost-cutting measure, reduced the rations issued to Indians it only added to their afflictions. By the early 1880s the miserable state of their people was forcing Indian leaders to press for renegotiation of the treaties.

White farmers had their own complaints. Then, as now, farmers believed they were getting a raw deal from Ottawa. They felt they were not getting a fair return for their produce, that tariffs protecting eastern industry artificially raised the price of farm machinery, and that they had no influence in Ottawa. Matters were not helped by the fact that there was an economic downturn in the late 1870s and early 1880s. The Prince Albert district was one of the more populated areas in the west and was the base of much of the farm discontent. It was there that the

Farmers' Union was founded in 1883.

William Henry Jackson was one of the founders of the movement. After spending three years at the University of Toronto, Jackson followed his settler parents to Prince Albert. In a small way Jackson took up farming, but his first love was politics. It was Jackson who acted as a liaison between the Farmers' Union and the Metis protest movement based in Batoche. In late 1884 Jackson and Riel collaborated in preparing a Bill of Rights which was sent to Ottawa. Jackson became so enamoured with the Metis cause that he moved to Batoche, Frenchified his name to Honoré Jaxon and converted to Catholicism. Later Jackson worked as Riel's secretary but, after a falling out, was jailed by the Metis leader. Following the Metis defeat at Batoche in May 1885, Jackson was tried as a conspirator but was found not guilty by reason of insanity.

Jackson's education served him well in his position as secretary of the Farmer's Union, a post in which he was responsible for documenting the farmers' grievances. Their demands were four: responsible government for the west; lower tariffs (farm machinery cost 40 per cent more on the Canadian prairies than it did in eastern Canada); cancellation of the monopoly granted to the CPR; and finally, construction of a railway to Hudson's Bay as a means of lowering transportation costs to the west.

A source of discontent for both Indians and whites was Edgar Dewdney, appointed lieutenant-governor of the Northwest Territories in 1881. Dewdney, a close friend of the Conservative government in Ottawa, ruled in an autocratic and arbitrary manner. He instituted the cut in rations for the Indians. He arranged for the move of the capital of the Northwest Territories from Battleford to Regina with amazing dispatch and little public consultation. In Regina, he quarrelled with the CPR over the exact location of the townsite. In the end Government House and the North-West Mounted Police headquarters ended up on Dewdney's land, some two miles away from the railway station.

Metis attempts to enlist the support of Indians and whites failed. In the case of the Indians, only a few bands joined the Metis at the outbreak of the rebellion. This was the result, partly of the desperate state of the Indians themselves, and partly of the prohibition of arms sales to Indians (instituted on March 12, 1885). Another factor was the influence of Catholic missionaries, who worked throughout the west convincing Indian bands not to take up arms. Many writers credit Father Albert Lacombe with convincing the Blackfoot to remain neutral.

As for the whites, the Farmer's Union was co-opted by Prince Albert's elite. Lawrence Clarke became an active member as did many other land speculators. The English-speaking Half-breed farmers generally sided with the Farmer's Union rather than with the French-speaking Metis. And when it came right down to it, most whites were not prepared to take up arms.

Nor did all the Metis support the rebellion. By and large, the fighting was confined to the Batoche area, which had one of the highest concentrations of Metis in the west. While the Metis in other areas were also unhappy with their lot, the presence of leaders like Gabriel Dumont, and later Riel, in Batoche helped the people unite against the government. In other areas, Catholic clergy such as Father Lacombe are believed to have played an important role in persuading the Metis not to take up arms.

Even in Batoche, the activists were largely hunters and labourers. Most of the merchants stayed neutral. Xavier Letendre, remarkably, collected $19,000 in reparations from the Rebellion Losses Commission for damage to his property during the rebellion. Other Batoche merchants like Solomon Venne, Georges Fisher and Jean-Bapiste Boyer were similarly compensated. The intellectuals, those members of the community who were educated and often held government jobs, stayed out too.

Rebellion

Although there is debate about the causes of the rebellion, everyone agrees that Louis Riel was a major player in it. Yet it was almost by accident that he appeared on the scene. He did not seek a role — history sought him out.

After Manitoba entered Confederation in 1870, Riel remained an influential figure among his people. When the Irish-American Fenians threatened St. Boniface in September 1871, Riel, by this time back at the Red River, was a member of the home guard. He was also active in politics, winning a federal by-election in 1873. On arriving in Ottawa, he decided against taking his seat in the House of Commons because of the inflamed feelings against him and the Metis. A federal election followed in 1874 and Riel again ran. After winning he intended to take up his seat; however, as soon as he took the oath of office he was expelled from the House on a motion introduced by the Ontario Orange leader, and later prime minister, Mackenzie Bowell.

Between 1876 and 1878 Riel spent time in two different mental asylums (as they were known then) in Quebec. There is uncertainty about the nature and extent, if any, of his illness. In 1878 he left Quebec and wandered through the eastern states. His wanderings took him farther west until eventually he reached Montana. There he became a trader and later took up a teaching position at St. Peter's Mission. He also met and married a Metis woman, Marguerite Monet, *dit* Bellehumeur, and they soon had two children.

While Riel was going peacefully about his affairs in Montana, things were heating up in the North-West. For several years, Gabriel Dumont had been the leader of the Metis council at Batoche. That body had repeatedly petitioned the government for redress of their grievances, but without any success.

Dumont was the grandson of a French-Canadian trader for the NWC and his Sarcee Indian wife. His father, Isadore, tried farming in the Red River area in the 1830s — Gabriel was born there in 1837 or 1838 — but gave up and moved west, eventually settling in the Batoche-St. Laurent region. As a young man, Gabriel was totally at home on the plains. He was an excellent shot, a skilled rider and a natural leader. His passion was the buffalo hunt, but he also ran a ferry south of Batoche and operated a store and poolroom.

Dumont had his weaknesses. He could not read or write and could barely speak English. Partly because of these handicaps, the council at Batoche-St. Laurent decided in March 1884 to seek out Riel's assistance. After making inquiries about Riel's whereabouts, a party led by Dumont set out for Montana. There they met with Riel and persuaded him to return. On July 1, 1884, the forty-year-old Riel arrived in Batoche.

His activities revolved around drawing up petitions and lists of demands. He was a popular speaker and addressed countless meetings of Indians, Metis and whites. Few whites feared him; in fact they hoped that his presence would in some way force Ottawa to act on western grievances. On September 19, 1884, the Prince Albert *Times* editorialized: "That there is anything in Mr. Riel's ability as leader to cause alarm is not believed by those who have had the opportunity of judging him...."

Yet Riel's presence in Batoche did not produce results — the federal government continued to stall on dealing with western grievances. By the end of 1884, Riel realized that there was nothing further he could do. He was prepared to leave. He asked the government to settle with him, first for his land in Manitoba (he had never claimed benefits under the Manitoba Act) and second for his service to Canada (heading the government in Manitoba from 1869-70). On February 20, 1885, Macdonald wrote to Lieutenant-Governor Dewdney, "we have no money to give to Riel and would be obliged to ask for a Parliamentary vote....How would it look to be obliged to confess we could not govern the country and were obliged to bribe a man to go away?" Riel received nothing.

By this time the tensions were such that armed conflict was inevitable. On March 18, Lawrence Clarke, returning from a trip to Ottawa, told the Metis of Batoche that on his way home he had met a contingent of five hundred North-West Mounted Police who were heading west. This report spread among the Metis; Dumont and his men seized all the guns and ammunition they could find in

Batoche's stores. The next day the Metis declared the formation of a new government with Pierre Parenteau as president and Gabriel Dumont as adjutant-general. Fourteen other men were included on the governing committee. Louis Riel was not a member.

Riel's exact role remains uncertain, but it is clear that he was an influential advisor to the Metis government — many of its documents included his signature. Yet he was no longer the man he once was. Suffering from a form of megalomania, he was obsessed with the notion that he had been chosen by God to create a new North American Catholicism. According to Father Vital Fourmond, who later provided evidence against Riel, Riel "...proclaimed himself a new Moses who had come to deliver his people from bondage...and he...would be crowned king of the world and sit in the chair of St. Peter at Rome, as the Pope...."

On March 25 the Metis raided several stores in Duck Lake in search of food. The following day a force of fifty-three police men and forty-seven armed civilians left Fort Carlton for Duck Lake to restore order. The Metis waited in ambush, hiding in trees surrounding the trail. Dumont and a group of Metis approached the police to talk; however, shots were fired (a civilian, Joe McKay, claimed he fired the first shot) and after the fighting was over five Metis were dead and so were twelve policemen and assistants. Eleven men were injured, some later dying of their wounds. Dumont's brother Isadore was killed and Gabriel himself was grazed at the temples and knocked off his horse. Dumont wanted to chase the police as they retreated, but Riel persuaded him to let them go, saying enough blood had been shed.

With war fever reaching a high pitch in the east, the federal government decided to send the army. The Indians acted too. On April 2 a band of Cree warriors from Big Bear's tribes raided the HBC store at Frog Lake in search of food. In the resulting skirmish nine white men, including the local Indian agent and two priests, died. Only the company's agent and two white women survived. News of this success encouraged other disgruntled Indian warriors in the Battleford area. Soon HBC stores at Fort Pitt, Lac La Biche, Cold Lake, Green Lake and Battleford were raided by starving Indians looking for food.

A lot had changed since 1870. In Manitoba, the Metis' tactic of establishing a government and increasing the pressure on Ottawa had succeeded for one simple reason — the Red River was a long way from Ottawa, and so the government had found it difficult to assert control. By 1885, however, the situation was different. The North-West was even more remote than the Red River, but by now the government had a railway to move troops quickly and efficiently. Seeing the rebellion as an ideal opportunity to prove its usefulness, the CPR promised to have troops in the west in eleven days. Thanks to the CPR and the heroic efforts of the militia to bridge the gaps in the unfinished railway in northern Ontario, troops were in western Canada in early April.

On April 6, a column of 800 men under the command of Major-General Frederick Middleton left the railway at Qu'Appelle and marched north. Several days later, 550 men moved north from Swift Current towards Battleford under the command of Lieutenant-Colonel William Otter. A third unit moved north from Calgary under the command of Major-General T.B. Strange. Dumont, who had fought hit-and-run battles against the Sioux along the Missouri, wanted to launch guerrilla attacks against the army. He also talked of blowing up the railway and attacking the troops in the Qu'Appelle valley. Riel would have none of it. He feared losing Dumont in a raid and also felt that such a campaign would leave Batoche undefended.

Eventually Dumont got his way and, on April 24, mounted a surprise attack on the army at Fish Creek, approximately twenty kilometres southwest of Batoche. In the day-long fight seven soldiers died and forty were injured. The Metis lost four men and another two were wounded. This battle set back the army's plans for a full two weeks. Before proceeding towards Batoche, the army waited for reinforcements, for a Gatling gun (forerunner of the machine gun) and for the steamer *Northcote* to be armed (it was to travel up the river and attack Batoche).

In the meantime, Otter's troops reached Battleford, which had been raided by Chief Poundmaker's Cree looking for food. At Cutknife Hill, Poundmaker's home territory, the troops surprised the Cree who scattered into the bushes and coulees and began firing at the troops on the bald hill above. As casualties mounted among the troops, Otter decided to withdraw. To his surprise he was able to withdraw unharassed; Poundmaker held his warriors back. The chief decided to march to Batoche, but by the time he arrived it had already fallen.

By this time Strange was pursuing the Cree while Middleton advanced on Batoche. There, the Metis dug rifle pits in the steep east bank of the South Saskatchewan River, constructing them so as to provide shelter from the army's fire. The engagement began on May 9. Outnumbered by at least four to one, the Metis quickly ran out of ammunition and were reduced to melting nails to make bullets. The resistance ended on May 12 when several companies of soldiers, in a move more spontaneous than planned, charged out of their trenches and overran the Metis position. The Metis fighters fled throughout the countryside.

The Making of a Martyr

After spending several days in the Batoche area, Gabriel Dumont fled to the United States. That option was open to Riel, but he chose to surrender on May 15. Almost immediately, he was transported to Regina. Chief Poundmaker surrendered on May 23 and Chief Big Bear on July 2. They were three of the nearly one hundred people arrested after the rebellion. Nearly seventy people were convicted on charges ranging from treason to theft. Big Bear and Poundmaker received three-year jail terms; both were released before the end of their terms and died within a year of their respective releases.

Riel was formally charged on July 6 with six counts of treason-felony under the 1352 English Statute of Treasons, the government claiming that he "did...maliciously and traitorously attempt and endeavour by force and arms to subvert and destroy the constitution and government of this realm...." The statute required the death penalty on conviction. (English law became the law of the Northwest Territories on July 25, 1870 — the day Canada took over the territories from the HBC).

The trial began on July 20, presided over by Stipendiary

Magistrate Hugh Richardson. Thirty-six persons were summoned as potential jurors, and six English Protestants were eventually selected. The next day the trial was adjourned for a week to allow defence witnesses to arrive from the east. The defence presented by Riel's lawyers, François-Xavier Lemieux and Charles Fitzpatrick, was one of insanity, a defence that Riel himself rejected.

On August 1, the jury, after deliberating for 1 1/2 hours, concluded that Riel was guilty but recommended that mercy be shown. The judge rejected the recommendation and, as required by law, sentenced Riel to hang.

The decision was appealed, first to the Manitoba Court of Queen's Bench and then to the Judicial Committee of the Privy Council (Canada's highest court of appeal until 1949) in London, England. Both bodies rejected Riel's appeal.

In Quebec, protests mounted. Macdonald feared that if Riel hanged he would lose his Quebec support, and so as a compromise he appointed a commission of three doctors to examine Riel's sanity. All historians agree that the exercise was a political farce. The three doctors chosen were Dr. Michael Lavell, warden of the Kingston Penitentiary and an obstetrician, Dr. François-Xavier Valade, an Ottawa doctor with party connections who was chosen because he was French-Canadian, and Dr. Augustus Jukes, the NWMP surgeon in Regina who had testified against Riel at his trial. Macdonald then wrote in secret to Lavell, explaining that he had told Valade that Lavell was an expert in psychiatry. He also told Lavell to stop his investigation as soon as "you are convinced Riel knows right from wrong."

Jukes wrote to the prime minister on November 6,

before the eastern doctors arrived, concluding that Riel was sane. Three days later he sent a caveat — there should be a further commission to examine Riel's writings. Lavell concluded that Riel was sane; Valade disagreed, saying that Riel was not "an accountable being...he is unable to distinguish between right and wrong...." Dewdney telegraphed the results and also added his assessment that the only difference between the reports was "a little difficulty about the phraseology...." The doctors were to write more detailed reports but Macdonald decided to proceed without waiting for them. On November 12, the cabinet decided that Riel should hang. When the matter was raised in the House of Commons in March 1886, falsified versions of the doctors' final reports were presented. Jukes' report was condensed so as to leave out his comments on Riel's eccentricities, and Valade's was significantly changed.

Riel was hanged on November 16. His body was taken to St. Boniface, where his funeral attracted hundreds of loyal followers. Many French-Canadians saw Riel's execution as an affront to them as a people, and for decades memories of the Macdonald government's action hovered over Canadian life like a dark shadow, contributing to the racial and religious tensions that are still part of our country's fabric.

Government Conspiracy?

There are people, such as Howard Adams and Don McLean, who see the 1885 rebellion as the result of a deliberate conspiracy on the part of the government. At this point their views do not enjoy wide acceptance. Most historians and political scientists, though they admit the legitimacy of the Metis' grievances, contend that the government's only crime was that of indifference to the west and its native inhabitants.

The conspiracy theory goes like this. By 1884 the CPR was on the verge of bankruptcy. Without the national railway, settlement in the west would be difficult; and without western settlement, there would be no market for eastern manufactured goods. The government had poured millions into the CPR and still the national railway had not been completed. Public protest was mounting against continued government expenditure on the project. To give more public money might bring about the defeat of the government; on the other hand, if the CPR went bankrupt, the dream of one nation from sea to sea would be shattered. Provoking a rebellion, say Adams and McLean, was one way of rallying support for the endangered CPR — a war would underline the need for a railway both to transport troops quickly to the west, and, in the long term, to maintain effective control over the region. This explains, they claim, why the government did nothing to address western grievances even though it received a stream of reports drawing attention to unrest in the region.

The government's need for a rebellion happened to coincide with the needs of certain interests in the west. After the location of the rail line was changed from the Prince Albert-Battleford-Edmonton route to a more southerly route running through Regina and Calgary, a depression hit the Prince Albert area. According to the conspiracy theory, a number of local business people helped provoke the rebellion in order to get the economy moving again. Police and soldiers stationed in the Prince Albert area would result in an increased demand for lodging, food, transportation and a variety of other services.

Lawrence Clarke was the chief provocateur. While Clarke overtly supported the Metis cause — he was the person chosen by the Metis to take their final petition to Ottawa in early 1885 — he was a government spy and, according to Adams and McLean, was persuaded by the government to provoke an incident. He did his job well. It is Adams' and McLean's contention that Clarke provoked the battle at Duck Lake, first by telling the police in Prince Albert that all was fine at Fort Carlton and there was no need for them to hurry to the scene, and then by goading the fort's commander, Major L.N.F. Crozier, into taking action against the Metis.

But Clarke was not alone. As an informer, one of his most important contacts was Father André, an ultra-conservative Oblate who always encouraged the Metis to vote for the Conservative Party. André made notes of who the protesters were, what they were saying and who took part in the uprising, and passed the information to the police and Clarke. Assisting him was Charles Nolin, a member of the provisional government, who, Adams alleges, made regular visits at odd hours of the night to André's presbytery.

Nolin, it is claimed, also played a role in provoking the rebellion. As an official of the provisional government, he allegedly encouraged the Metis to take up arms. However, his colleagues became suspicious of his activities and had him arrested and tried on a charge of treason.

He was sentenced to death but was spared that fate because of the intervention of the clergy. Nolin was a Crown witness at the trials which followed the rebellion and was later appointed a magistrate.

The idea of a conspiracy is a new one. Whether it will survive detailed historical analysis remains to be seen. At this point, there is not enough evidence to make a final judgment. And perhaps, in view of the fact that many documents are missing and much uncertainty surrounds the events of 1885, a final judgment will never be possible. Still, the conduct of Macdonald's government just prior to and during the rebellion does raise suspicions. If there was a conspiracy, this fact would lend great support to the Metis' claim that the federal government has a legal responsibility to redress their grievances.

Legal Consequences of Military Defeat

What were the legal consequences of military defeat for Metis rights?

First, some salient facts should be highlighted. Under international law all rights of a defeated nation continue in force until such time as the conquering power has taken those rights by an official act or declaration. A similar concept applies in domestic law. Conviction for a criminal offence does not mean the loss of all one's rights. For example, a conviction for a treasonous offence does not deprive the guilty party of his or her property, unless there is a specific law taking away those rights. The question, then, is whether the Canadian government did anything after the rebellion to strip the Metis of their rights. The answer is simply that it did not. In fact, the government did the opposite — it took several steps towards recognizing Metis rights. After the rebellion, the scrip system was put into operation to satisfy Metis claims. Similarly, in 1889-90, much of the Batoche area was resurveyed into riverlots. The conquering power, far from taking away rights, made an effort to recognize them.

Secondly, if rights are indeed lost by military defeat (or through conviction for a criminal offence), this principle should apply only to those Metis who actively took part in the rebellion. By and large, most Metis in western Canada did not take part in the rebellion. Even in Batoche, where most of the fighting took place, the merchants and intellectuals stayed on the sidelines.

There is another legal point, too. If, as Howard Adams and Don McLean argue, the government was actively involved in provoking the rebellion, the question arises whether it can be called to account for its actions. Precedents exist. The government has entered into negotiations with Canadians of Japanese origin to compensate them for wrongs committed in World War II, when they were forcefully moved from the west coast and their property expropriated without compensation. Of course, the decision to enter into negotiations is a political, not legal, matter.

The Metis, however, may have a legal claim against the government. Many people argue the government has a trust or fiduciary relationship to native people to act in their best interest. The concept of a trust relationship stems from the 1985 Supreme Court of Canada decision in the Guerin case. The issue was a decision by the Department of Indian Affairs to lease reserve land in

Vancouver to a golf club on very favourable terms. Eventually, the Indian band sued the federal government for the financial loss it had suffered because the lease tied up valuable property in Vancouver for a long time at bargain-basement prices. The Supreme Court found that the federal government had a legal responsibility to ensure that it obtained the best possible financial deal for Indian people when dealing with their land. The full implications of this decision are the source of much debate among legal scholars, lawyers, government officials and native leaders. It will probably require several more decisions from the Supreme Court before the full extent of the government's duty is known.

However, the case raises interesting questions for Metis claims. Does the federal government have a similar responsibility to the Metis? If the government in fact played a role in provoking the rebellion, its actions were clearly a breach of its trust relationship. Even if there was no conspiracy there is certainly evidence that the government was, through negligence and lack of judgment, partly responsible for the rebellion. Is this, too, not a breach of trust? The possibility thus exists that the federal government may one day have to settle with the Metis for its conduct prior to and during the rebellion.

5
Broken Promises

In the years following the rebellion, the economic and political circumstances of the Metis changed drastically. Buffalo and wild game became scarce, making it more difficult to live off the land. Critically, the fur trade, in which many Metis earned their livelihood, became an insignificant industry as settlers took over the west. The resulting unemployment and death of a way of life carried serious consequences. Historian Diane Payment has concluded:

> There is evidence that many young men in the community turned to liquor in these difficult transitional years of few jobs and social ostracization of the "descendants of the rebels"....Tuberculosis reached almost epidemic proportions at the turn of the century, weakening the general health of surviving family members. "Accidental" deaths, "troubled" minds, abandonment of families, and a variety of petty crimes, were on the increase in a society disrupted by too rapid social change and foreign values.

The changing economic circumstances of the Metis also contributed to an absence of political action. As the

Metis slipped into poverty, dependent upon the government and church to survive, political activism became difficult to sustain. Poor people rarely become political activists.

Of course, the death of political activism among the Metis was also the product of their military defeat in 1885. Prior to then, every time the Metis had fought they had achieved some success. They had emerged victorious at the Battle of Seven Oaks; they had won the free-trade fight against the HBC; and in 1870 they had forced the government to create a new province. But in 1885 they were defeated, their military leaders had fled and they had no military or negotiating power to force the government to address their grievances. It was fifty years later, in Alberta, before the Metis again took up the struggle for the recognition of their rights.

That renewed struggle was prompted in part by the problems which arose from the federal government's scrip system. Based to a large extent on a similar system used in Manitoba, it was the system adopted by the federal government to deal with the Metis land claims after the rebellion. Not surprisingly, the problems it created in Manitoba also cropped up on the prairies.

What is Scrip?

The dictionary defines "scrip" as a certificate which entitles the bearer to receive something — land, money, shares — at a later date upon presentation of the certificate. And in western Canada in the late 1800s that was what the federal government did; it issued "scrip" certificates entitling the bearer to either a specified acreage of land or a sum of money which could be applied to the purchase of land. Scrip certificates were issued to individual Metis to satisfy their claim to land entitlement.

The use of the scrip system was not confined to the Metis. Scrip certificates were issued in 1873 to the original white settlers in Manitoba and were later issued to reward volunteers who fought in 1885, veterans of the Boer War and officers of the North West Mounted Police. The largest scrip issues, however, were to the Metis and these generated the most controversy.

The certificates looked like government bonds and were printed by the Canadian Bank Note Company in denominations of $80, $160 and $240. Land scrip certificates were issued for 80 acres, 160 acres or 240 acres. (Initially, the government proceeded on the assumption that one acre was worth one dollar). Land scrip certificates allowed the bearer to go to a Dominion land titles office and claim land which was available for settlement, the amount being determined by the acres prescribed in the certificate.

A typical land scrip certificate read:

DOMINION OF CANADA
DEPARTMENT OF THE INTERIOR

This Scrip note is receivable as payment in full for
ONE HUNDRED and SIXTY ACRES
Of Dominion Lands, open for ordinary Homestead only if presented by _____
at the office of Dominion Lands of the District within which such lands are situated in conformity with Scrip Certificate form _____ granted by the

North West Half Breed Commission this _____ day of _____ 18____.

A typical money scrip certificate read:

DOMINION OF CANADA
DEPARTMENT OF THE INTERIOR

In conformity with Certificate form No. _____ granted by the North West Half Breed Commission It Is Hereby Certified that under the authority of an order of the Honorable the Privy Council dated _____ of _____ 18____ as amended by the order of _____ of _____ 18____, and in accordance with the provisions of subsec. (e), Sec. 81, 46 Vic. Cap.17_____, a Half-Breed, is entitled to TWO HUNDRED AND FORTY DOLLARS IN SCRIP. The coupons attached to this will be accepted in payment of Dominion Lands on presentation at the office of Dominion Lands of the District within which such lands are situated.

Issued at the Department of the Interior, Ottawa, this _____ of _____, 18____.

From time to time changes were made in the wording of the scrip certificates. The legal effect, however, remained the same.

The Legal Framework for the Scrip System

As already explained, the government laid the ground-work for addressing Metis claims with an 1879 amend-ment to the Dominion Lands Act and a further amend-ment in 1883. During the same period, to accommodate Metis who had joined Indians in signing treaties, the Indian Act was amended to allow those Metis to with-draw from treaties and take scrip instead, the only stipu-lation being that they return all treaty money they had received (this requirement was eventually abolished). Later, in January 1885, an order-in-council empowered the government to enumerate Metis who might be eli-gible for a land grant. However, action was delayed until March 30, 1885, four days after the battle of Duck Lake, when a commission was appointed to enumerate and deal with Metis claims. The commissioners were authorized to deal with all Metis who lived in areas where treaties had been signed by Indians (essentially all of the southern prairies). Their instructions were to give land scrip to Metis who were in bona fide and undisputed occupation of land. Money scrip was to be granted to those not in occupation. Land scrip was to be 240 acres for children and 160 acres for adults; money scrip was in the amount of $240 for children and $160 for adults. By April 7, 1885 the commission was in the field carrying out its work.

Between April 10 and August 28 the commission visited Winnipeg, Regina, Moose Jaw, Willow Bunch, Fort Qu'Appelle, Calgary, Edmonton, Prince Albert, and Cumberland House. It allowed 1,678 of 1,815 claims. Money scrip worth $279,000 and land scrip covering 55,260 acres was issued. The commission was instructed to reserve decision on any claims made by participants in the 1885 rebellion. It is not known whether any final decision was made on these claims.

The 1885 commission could not handle all Metis claims. As a result, three other commissions were appointed to handle those claimants and areas missed in 1885. Their work was confined to dealing with Metis in areas where treaties had been signed with Indians.

Later, other commissions were appointed to deal with Metis claims in northern Alberta, Saskatchewan, Manitoba and what is now the Northwest Territories. These commissions worked in conjunction with Indian commissioners who were negotiating treaties with Indians.

In the period 1885 to 1921, twelve Half-Breed Commissions travelled the west and north to enumerate Metis and issue scrip. All were established by federal orders-in-council and their powers varied. Until 1899 the commissions could deal only with individuals who had been born prior to July 15, 1870. The 1899 scrip commission was empowered to deal with claimants born prior to December 31, 1885. After 1900, the cutoff date for scrip eligibility was determined by the date on which a treaty was signed with the local Indians. Treaty 10, for example, covering much of northern Saskatchewan, was signed in 1906, meaning that all Metis in the Treaty 10 area born before 1906 qualified for scrip. Of course, there were many exceptions to the general powers summarized here, and these exceptions made ineligible some claimants who were born before the cut-off date.

The twelve commissions allowed over 13,200 claims with approximately two-thirds of the scrip being issued for money and the balance for land. Because of the difficulty in determining the size of the Metis population, and in view of the complexities of the scrip system, it is impossible to say what percentage of the Metis population claimed scrip.

The Scrip System in Operation

The rules regarding scrip could best be described as an historian's nightmare and a puzzle solver's dream. In the period 1871-1925 the federal cabinet issued some 120 orders-in-council dealing with the scrip system in Manitoba and the prairies, in addition to several amendments to the Dominion Lands Act made by Parliament. On top of this legal structure were various Department of the Interior policy decisions dealing with scrip. On occasion, these policy decisions contradicted the law. In May 1900 the federal Deputy Minister of Justice wrote:

> ...it is not in my opinion necessary that in awarding scrip the rules of law governing the devolution of intestates' estates [laws governing what happens when one dies without a will] should be strictly followed...I think it is competent for the Governor in Council...to adopt such rules as he may think proper....

Among the rules established were that:

- while money scrip entitled a person to buy land, it was personal property and did not have to be registered in

the land titles office
- powers of attorney for money scrip would be recognized
- next-of-kin were entitled to a deceased's scrip claim
- minors could not assign land scrip, but they could assign money scrip
- land scrip was not assignable; the land had to be claimed by the Metis claimant personally
- a guardian could claim land under a land scrip for a minor
- the Department of the Interior had no responsibility to investigate charges of fraud

Today, many of these rules are the subject of debate and may end up being crucial points in future litigation. The federal position is that the rules were designed for the protection of the Metis.

The 1885 scrip commission had three members: William Street, a lawyer from London, Ontario, acted as chairman; Roger Goulet, a Metis surveyor from St. Boniface; and Regina lawyer Amédée Forget. Subsequent commissions varied in membership from one to three individuals.

Procedures followed by each commission were largely the same. All acted on instructions from the Department of the Interior and each had the power to call witnesses and to take sworn testimony.

Commissions travelled to communities in their assigned geographic areas. In advance of their travels a schedule of hearings was established and advertised in area newspapers. (It should be borne in mind that in the 1880s and 1890s there were few newspapers in the west and, more important, few Metis who could read English).

Notices of the hearings were also posted in church halls, trading posts and land titles offices. Government workers, traders and the clergy were asked to pass word of the hearings to Metis they met.

Commissioners travelled with a retinue of staff, including secretaries and clerks, cooks, labourers and interpreters. The latter were necessary because many Metis spoke no English, the language of all proceedings. In most cases the interpreters were other Metis. Father Lacombe, who worked with the 1899 commission and received remuneration of ten dollars a day for his labours, recorded in his diary that fifty people, including eleven policemen, travelled with that commission.

The commissions set out on their travels in early spring and continued their work until late fall. Travel was by horse, foot and boat. Occasionally the schedule was upset by weather.

It was the responsibility of the individual Metis to present themselves before the commission to advance their claims. Tents were set up at the advertised locations and equipped with chairs and tables at which the commissioners sat to take applications and hear evidence. Photos show the commissioners usually wearing jackets and ties.

Charles Mair, one of the secretaries to the 1899 commission, gave this account in his book *Through the MacKenzie Basin: A Narrative of the Athabasca and Peace River Treaty Expedition of 1899*: "The 'scrip tent', as it was called, a large marquee fitted up as an office, had been pitched with the other tents when the camp was made, and in this the half-breeds held a crowded meeting to talk over terms, and to collate their own opinions as to the form of scrip issue they most desired."

The claimants had many things to discuss. First, they had to decide whether to take scrip or to become treaty Indians. If they chose the second option they would receive treaty money and all other benefits available to treaty Indians. They could not have both scrip and treaty benefits. The Indian Act specifically barred (and continues to bar) anyone who received "half-breed scrip" from being registered as an Indian.

Historians disagree on whether the Metis had a choice between money and land scrip and what their decisions were. Some writers, like Thomas Flanagan, argue that the Metis wanted money scrip. They needed cash and saw money scrip as a quicker way to get it. Others argue that the Metis wanted land but the government was afraid of tying up large blocks of land for the Metis and therefore convinced them to take money scrip. In their study, *Metis Land Rights in Alberta: A Political History*, the Metis Association of Alberta gives this example:

> The use of land scrip came about because of demands from the Half-breeds, clergy and others for actual land grants as opposed to scrip. Apparently land scrip was seen as a compromise. For example, in 1885 the Half-breeds of the Qu'Appelle Lakes refused to accept money scrip certificates for their approved applications. As a result of this demand the Half-breed children who were eligible for a grant were given the option of taking either money scrip for $240, or land scrip for 240 acres of Dominion Lands. The heads of Half-breed families, however, were only entitled to money scrip.

Claimants were dealt with on an individual basis. Applications had to be supported by documentation to confirm identity as well as place and date of birth. The commission had to satisfy itself that the individual was a Metis and was born prior to the cutoff date. He or she also had to prove residence in the geographic area covered by the commission. Sometimes these facts were proved by sworn statement, other times documents such as baptism records had to be produced, and on yet other occasions witnesses would be called to give sworn testimony. Previous scrip records were checked to see if the claimant had received scrip before. Again Charles Mair reports: "This was a slow process, involving in every case a careful search of the five elephant folios containing the records of the bygone issues of scrip in Manitoba and the organized Territories."

One of three decisions was made on each claim. It was either accepted, deferred (often sent to Ottawa for decision) or rejected. If a claim was accepted a document was issued to the claimant. This had to be sent to the Department of the Interior which would issue the actual scrip certificate. Money scrip certificates could be sold or exchanged for land at the land titles office.

What Actually Happened

There is no question that the Metis did not end up owning large amounts of land as a result of the scrip system. Nor is there any dispute that speculators made significant profits on lands supposedly destined to settle Metis claims. According to research carried out by the Association of Metis and Non-Status Indians of Saskatchewan,

90 per cent of scrip certificates ended up in the hands of bankers, lawyers and merchants, bought at prices ranging from 25 to 33 per cent of face value.

The extent of the traffic in scrip certificates is also well documented in the research carried out by the Regina-based, Metis-controlled Gabriel Dumont Institute. In its Metis Historical Collection the institute has recorded, in massive black binders, every scrip certificate, who it was issued to and what became of it. Volume 76D lists money scrips issued in 1886 to people with surnames between L and Z. Of these, 346 certificates were issued to people with names beginning with L and M. A random search shows that 33 of the 346 were eventually owned by Osler and Hammond, Toronto financial agents. The Merchants Bank of Winnipeg acquired 38. Winnipeg bankers W.F. Alloway and H.T. Champion — former soldiers who had been part of Colonel Wolseley's expedition in 1870 — obtained 23. And the list goes on. It is clear that very few Metis ended up using their scrip certificates to buy land.

Why did this happen? To answer that question several others have to be raised. Were the Metis aware of what they were doing when they sold their certificates at a discount? Were the prices they were paid for the certificates outrageously low? Did they actively solicit buyers for their certificates? Was large-scale fraud committed against the Metis to deprive them of their scrip benefits? Did the government know about this fraud? Did the government encourage the fraudulent practices?

Definitive answers will probably never be found. Don McLean says that "so many documents have been destroyed that there can only be circumstantial evidence." Thomas Flanagan takes a different view, stating flatly that the Metis were not in any way defrauded or duped. He argues that the Metis were skilled traders and often bargained intently with purchasers of their scrips (the counter argument is that the Metis' business acumen related to the fur trade, and they had no experience in land dealings or transactions which were governed by extensive documentation). Flanagan also argues, and many other historians agree with him, that the poverty-stricken Metis were in need of quick cash and the sale of scrip was one way to raise money quickly. Finally, he asserts that there was competition amongst the buyers and that to date no evidence of a conspiracy by speculators or the government has been uncovered.

Flanagan's argument receives some support from a letter written by D.H. MacDowall, a Member of Parliament from the Saskatchewan district. In 1892 MacDowall wrote to Prime Minister J.J.C. Abbott telling him that prosperous Metis used their scrip certificates to obtain land but poor ones were forced to sell their scrip quickly to satisfy creditors.

The Metis argue that the government was well aware that speculation in Metis scrip was rampant and did nothing to stop it. They say that speculators often travelled in advance of the scrip commission urging the Metis to lobby for scrip. Sometimes they took powers of attorney for scrip certificates which had not yet been issued. On other occasions the speculators travelled with the commission, or followed after it, buying up scrip. Many of the Metis signed documents presented to them by the speculators not understanding what they were signing. Sometimes the powers of attorney were signed without the forms being completed. Promises were made for payments, but the payment was often not forthcoming.

R.A. Ruttan, of the Edmonton Dominion Lands office, expressed his conclusions in a 1896 letter to his superiors in Winnipeg:

> Brokers hoping to make money out of the scrip are agitating for a supplemental grant. They hope to excite the Half-Breed to an interest in the matter by agreeing to purchase....In the meanwhile the brokers are getting these powers of attorney signed by the prospective beneficiaries. To the execution of the instrument the Half-Breed will be lured by an assurance that it is a "petition" or "census form"....the present process is much like the old one under which these people were swindled right and left and everywhere to the fullest extent. I do not believe that the Half-Breed allottee benefitted to the extent of 20 per cent of the original grant.

Similarly, in 1900 two scrip commissioners, investigating Metis claims in Saskatchewan, found that many powers of attorney had been obtained years in advance of their sitting and in many cases there was no — or minimal — compensation paid to the Metis concerned. They concluded that the Metis "were ignorant of the purport of the documents they had been induced to sign and which they most emphatically repudiate."

In getting around the rule that land scrip was nonassignable, speculators were particularly devious. As already noted, only the person named in the certificate could claim the land, and to do so he or she had to appear at the Dominion Lands office. Metis vendors of scrip, as

part of the sale, were required to accompany the speculator to the land titles office to complete the necessary
documentation. Payment to the Metis would be completed when this requirement was met. Sometimes,
however, any willing Metis would be hired to accompany
a speculator to the land titles office, fraudulently claiming
to be the person named in the scrip certificate. Prior to the
visit to the land titles office the claimant, real or fraudulent, would sign a transfer of all his rights to the speculator
and, once the title was issued to the claimant, it was
immediately turned over to the speculator. J.A. McK-
enna, an Indian Affairs officer who also headed up
several scrip commissions, wrote to the Minister of the
Interior on June 14, 1901, in these terms:

> ...it is not a hard matter to get half-breeds who will go
> before an Agent [at a Dominion Lands Office] to
> whom they are unknown and will be prepared to
> declare that they are the parties mentioned in the
> scrips and make the necessary declarations [to obtain
> the land].

The courts helped the speculators in finding loopholes
in the non-assignability of land scrip rule. In the early
1900s the Manitoba Court of King's Bench dealt with
Mrs. Battley's case. She had sold several scrip certificates to a Mr. McMeans who in turn resold it to other
people. In December 1903 Battley went to the land titles
office at Wapella with a Mr. Wright who now owned the
certificates — her presence was necessary as, by law, the
title could be issued only to her. Once Wright placed the
certificates on the land titles desk Battley took off with

them. Wright sued for their return. Battley argued that, since assignments of land scrip were not valid, Wright had no legal right to them and could not by law claim the land. If he could not claim the land, Battley's lawyer argued, Wright also had no right to the certificate. The court ruled in Wright's favour, declaring that the certificate was not land and therefore it was assignable. Battley's only remedy was to refuse to go to the land titles office to make her claim — this would mean that Wright could not get the land (unless he found someone to go in and claim she was Battley). She could not, however, get her certificate back.

A decade later the Exchequer Court of Canada came to a similar conclusion. In 1900 twenty-two-year-old Antoine L'Hirondelle received a scrip certificate entitling him to 240 acres of land. His father, Jean Baptiste L'Hirondelle, asked his son to give him this certificate so he could pay a debt of $500 he owed to the firm of McDougall and Secord. The son agreed and the father gave the certificate to his creditors. They credited the father's account with the going rate of $150.

The certificate was exchanged for land in 1902, but the son denied that he had signed the necessary documents at the land titles office. John McDougall testified that he often paid a half-breed between ten and fifteen dollars to go to the land titles office, but the evidence was unclear whether he had in this case.

In 1916 the son sued the Crown for the return of his certificate, alleging that because the certificate was non-assignable only he could benefit from it. The court ruled that the government had satisfied its obligation by issuing the certificate and owed no further obligation to the son. What the son did with his certificate was his own business.

On the same day the court also dealt with Joseph L'Hirondelle's claim. Joseph was Antoine's younger brother who had also given his father his land scrip certificate. That certificate, too, was given to McDougall and Secord to satisfy indebtedness. The only difference was that Joseph was a minor when he handed over his certificate. Regardless, the court disposed of Joseph's case just as it had his brother's.

The L'Hirondelle and Battley cases clearly illustrate that there was an active traffic in scrip certificates. They also belie the government's contention that the rule of non-assignment of land scrip was sufficient to protect Metis rights.

There were many public protests against these practices. Father Lacombe wrote to the Winnipeg Free Press in 1896:

> The law of the land would not permit a man to retain property taken from a minor; but it allows sharks to use legal devices to rob unwary people of their property. No sooner did it become known that the government of Canada contemplated issuing scrip to half-breeds, then the sharks set to work to devise safe means to rob them.

In its study *Metis Land Rights in Alberta: A Political History*, the Metis Association of Alberta alleges that the government openly abetted the traffic in scrip. It says that Dominion Land Offices ran accounts for speculators, who could deposit scrip they had purchased at the land office for safe-keeping and draw on these certificates when required for payment of land. It further alleges that land offices posted lists of local speculators, thus enabling land buyers to determine who might have scrip for sale. As authority, they cite correspondence from the Secretary of the Department of the Interior to various merchants and bankers in the west. The association's conclusions are supported by research carried out by the Association of Metis and Non-Status Indians of Saskatchewan. Clem Chartier, a former president of the World Council of Indigenous People and a lawyer, speaking at a 1983 conference on behalf of the Association of Metis and Non-Status Indians of Saskatchewan, stated:

> Over 90 per cent of the scrip was delivered into the hands of banks and speculators. The banks received over 52 per cent of the issued scrip. The Department of the Interior, which was responsible for the scrip program, facilitated the transfer of scrip to corporations and individual speculators by keeping scrip accounts for them.

In 1911 the Metis of Lesser Slave Lake petitioned the Minister of the Interior, Frank Oliver, to set up a Royal Commission to investigate "the frauds, schemes, false representations, deceit, perjury and forgery in connection with the issue and application of Half-breed scrips in the Northern Portion of Alberta...." In reply, they were told that they would have to prove fraud before the government would take any action.

In 1920 several Alberta Metis drew up a petition to Prime Minister Arthur Meighen asking for a royal commission to investigate scrip fraud. Meighen replied that scrip was issued to individuals and the government could bear no responsibility for what people did with the certificates. Aggrieved individuals, Meighen continued, could go to court to seek justice.

Prompted by Meighen's statement, one Metis did just that in 1921. John Graham of Wabasca, a Metis political activist who was involved in fighting for justice for his people, laid a charge of forgery against Richard Secord based on a 1903 incident. The allegation was that Secord bribed a Metis woman to go to the Edmonton land titles office and claim she was Elizabeth Hyslop, in whose name a scrip certificate for 240 acres had been issued. The fraudulent Hyslop was alleged to have received ten dollars and a shawl to make her mark on an application for land based on the Hyslop scrip certificate. Her mark on the application was witnessed by Richard Secord, who had accompanied her to the land office. Nine days later the land was sold to John McDougall and Richard Secord.

Secord was remanded for trial after a preliminary hearing and released on five thousand dollars bail. Before the case could come before the court, Parliament passed an amendment to the Criminal Code placing a three-year limitation period on prosecutions for offences relating to land purchased by "half-breed" scrip. Senator James Lougheed, then Minister of the Interior and grandfather of Peter Lougheed, guided the bill through the Senate. The result of the amendment was that prosecution against Secord was halted because the alleged fraud had occurred seventeen years earlier.

As further research is carried out by historians, legal researchers and Metis political organizations the list of suspicious circumstances will grow. For now, it is clear that the ancestors of a great many present-day Metis took scrip at one time. A few actually received land, a great many more sold their scrip, and many of the sales were at less than market value. The Metis were selling off their land for a song.

There can also be no question that outright fraud was committed against some Metis. All that remains unknown is the extent of the fraud.

The Metis are right in believing that the governments of the day were aware of some of the suspicious dealings which were occurring with regard to Metis scrip. Why then did it not change the system to ensure that Metis interests were protected? There were many ways in which government could have improved the situation. For example, rather than granting scrip to individuals, land could have been set aside for Metis communities with the title remaining in trust with the federal government. Or government could have tightened up the scrip rules to ensure that the Metis ended up owning land. Did the government's inaction mean that it was actively involved in defrauding the Metis, or was it simply turning a blind eye in the belief that the Metis would not make good farmers and it would be better if the land ended up in the hands of white European settlers? The verdict is not yet in.

As a means of settling Metis land claims, it is clear that the scrip system was a failure. It did not put land into the hands of the Metis, nor did it leave the Metis feeling that they had been fairly dealt with. Had another scheme been tried, perhaps today's political agenda would be different.

What Does Scrip Mean Today?

It is entirely possible that in the not too distant future the scrip system will be the basis of litigation. The federal government takes the position that, if the Metis had aboriginal title, their claim was satisfied by land granted under the terms of the Manitoba Act and the scrip system. The Metis respond that the scrip system did not deal with the land claims. First, they argue that not all Metis were eligible to benefit under the scrip system — cut-off dates, complex rules and the need for documentary evidence denied scrip to many Metis. Second, of those Metis who were eligible, few actually received the land benefits to which they were entitled — thanks in part to the fraud perpetrated against them.

Even if the government's assertion that it has dealt with Metis claims is correct, a further legal question arises. Does the 1985 Supreme Court decision in the Guerin case — that the federal government has a trust obligation to Indian people — apply to the Metis as well? If it does, did the Metis obtain the most favourable deal for their land rights through the scrip system? If the federal government actively colluded or even if it only turned a blind eye while speculators exploited the Metis, it clearly breached its trust obligations.

Another fact supporting the Metis position is that the scrip system was implemented without consultation or negotiation. The Metis were not asked if they wanted land to be granted to them as a group or as individuals. Nor were their individual scrips granted so that they could settle as a block. During the same period the federal government dealt with the Indians as a group, negotiated treaties with them and created reserves where they could live as communities. In the case of both the Indians and the Metis the government objective was the same — the extinguishment of aboriginal title. Why, then, did the government adopt radically different policies in dealing with the two groups?

The last scrip certificate was issued in 1923. But issues surrounding the scrip system still face Canada and will continue to do so. The Metis seek a land base on which they can govern themselves and through which they can protect their culture. Should the scrip issue be renegotiated?

Opponents argue that to renegotiate scrip is only to open up a round of problems that would plague Canada for another century. On the other hand, the Metis have made it clear that they will not forget questions surrounding the issue of scrip. The subject cannot be ignored. And as evidence continues to mount, it is plain that there is a strong moral case — and possibly even a legal one — for reviewing the sorry history of the scrip system.

6

Alberta's Metis Settlements

Two hundred kilometres northeast of Edmonton, in Alberta's rolling bush country, a sign along highway 36 reads:

> FISHING, HUNTING AND TRAPPING PROHIBITED
> By Persons other than members of Kikino
> Colony and bona fide residents of Kikino
> Metis Colony. Alberta Reg. 115/60 -116/60
> Violators are liable on summary conviction to
> $100 fine or 90 days Imprisonment
> DEPARTMENT OF MUNICIPAL AFFAIRS

Little of the hilly country is cleared; stands of tall poplars are interspersed with equally tall spruce. Every few kilometres there is a clearing and a house. Luxury houses, the kind found in an upper-middle-class residential neighbourhood, stand in marked contrast to the small rectangular bungalows, many in need of paint and repairs. The bungalows are predominant and are reminiscent of the housing built by the Department of Indians Affairs on reserves during the 1950s and 1960s.

Further up the road is the turnoff to the hamlet of Kikino, a cluster of some fifty houses and the only urban centre in the settlement. The houses resemble those found along the highway; several luxury log cabins (the pricey kind one expects to see at an exclusive lake resort) among a larger number of small bungalows.

On a rise overlooking the settlement stands a war memorial dedicated to the two men from the hamlet who gave their lives in the two world wars. There is little obvious commercial activity. There are, however, a lot of children playing in the quiet streets, where every strange car gets a wave and more than a second look. There is a kindergarten to serve the children, across the street from the garage which houses the settlement's fire truck. Farther down the road is a hydrant, evidence of the hamlet's running-water system, something that is still considered a luxury in some prairie communities. The two flag poles in front of the house next to the kindergarten are a sure sign that it has been converted to an office. The sign on the house indicates that this is the office of the Kikino Metis Settlement Association.

The Kikino settlement, covering approximately 180 square miles and with a population of nearly seven hundred, is one of eight Metis settlements in Alberta, all located in the north-central part of the province. According to provincial reports, the four northwestern settlements (Big Prairie, East Prairie, Keg River and Utikuma Lake) are largely agricultural, whereas the four northeastern settlements (Caslan, Elizabeth Lake, Fishing Lake and Kikino) are primarily grazing land and woodland. In recent years a number of the settlements have started game ranching (domestication of game), which has proven to be a profitable enterprise. All the settlements derive some revenue from leasing surface rights to oil companies.

The eight settlements cover a total of 2,000 square miles (1.25 million acres) and have a total population of 4,000. Each settlement is an independent unit with its own administration. Initially, the settlements were truly colonies with all administration in the hands of provincially appointed officials. Over the years some responsibility has devolved from Edmonton to the settlements, and the process of decentralization has reached a stage where the settlements have been offered a municipal form of self-government.

A provincial organization, the Alberta Federation of Metis Settlement Associations, was formed in 1975 to lobby and represent the interests of all the settlements. It has played an important role in the 1980s in the fight to secure constitutional protection for settlement lands and a greater measure of self-government.

The First Settlement

The idea of forming settlements for the Metis was conceived in the last quarter of the 19th century as an alternative to the disastrous scrip system. Among those who suggested it were Father Albert Lacombe, Archbishop Taché, the Metis of Cypress Hills and D.H. MacDowall, a federal Member of Parliament representing the Saskatchewan district of the Northwest Territories. It was Lacombe, however, who turned the idea to reality.

By the early 1890s Lacombe had worked with native people for almost four decades, and he was genuinely concerned about their social and economic circumstances. He had a particular soft spot for the Metis, perhaps because his grandmother was half-Indian, but also because he saw them as the vanguard of a burgeoning French Catholic society which he hoped would fill the west. Deeply angered by the speculation in Metis scrip, he wrote in his diary: "The Metis are doomed. They have sold their lands for a song; they are children and they have been reduced to poverty." To help the Metis, in 1895 he devised a plan for a farming colony. In his proposal called "A Philanthropic Plan to Redeem the Half-breeds of Manitoba and the North West Territories", each Metis family would be given a lifetime grant of eighty acres of land. Title would remain with the Oblate Fathers, the order to which Lacombe belonged. Seed and implements would be provided to the farmers, and the Church would build a school for the children.

At this time Lacombe was — thanks to his success over the years in pacifying western Indian tribes — a man of considerable influence in Ottawa, often sought out by cabinet ministers and even prime ministers for his views on western affairs. Not surprisingly, therefore, his plan received a favourable reception in government circles. In late 1895 the federal government granted the Oblates a twenty-one-year lease of four townships of land (144 square miles) in what is now northeastern Alberta, at an annual rental of two dollars per year. In addition, the government granted two thousand dollars for the purchase of seeds and implements. Lacombe printed a brochure in English, French and Cree extolling the virtues of the colony, which he named St. Paul des Métis, and distributed it among the Metis. The CPR offered free transportation for Metis moving to the settlement. Father A. Thérien, another Oblate, was put in charge of the settlement, with Lacombe confining his efforts to raising money for it. In fact, Lacombe visited the settlement only three times.

The settlement was beset with difficulties from the start. Few Metis moved there — in its first two years of existence it managed to attract only thirty-two families — and it was plagued by crop failures and a constant shortage of cash. In its study *Metis Land Rights in Alberta: A Political History*, the Metis Association of Alberta claims that the Oblates had unrealistic plans for the settlement. It argues that too much money was put into building an impressive four-storey boarding school, and not enough into economic development. It also argues that the settlement's difficulties stemmed from a failure on the part of the Oblates to involve the residents in decision-making.

The final blow came in January 1905 when the school burned down; the fire had been deliberately set by some of the students. From that point on the Oblates worked towards winding down the colony. French Canadian squatters were allowed to take up residence, and at the same time Thérien tried to convince the Metis of the settlement to leave. The Oblates and the government began secret discussions aimed at opening the settlement to homesteading, with the priests determined to retain control so as to ensure that the area remained French and Catholic. In early 1909, with little public notice, the land was opened to homesteading. The Oblates, with the cooperation of federal officials, arranged for some 250 pre-selected French Canadians to make their claim in advance of anyone else. While a number of Metis claims were allowed prior to the land being opened for homesteading, an equal number were denied.

Some of the dispossessed Metis moved to the Fishing Lake area, where they squatted on unoccupied Crown lands. Several decades later their justified fear that the land would be opened for homesteading led these Metis to lobby for a new settlement.

New Leadership

The 1930s were mean times on the prairies. A combination of economic depression, crop failure and drought left much of the population in third-world conditions. Wheat, for which there was no market, was roasted to make coffee. Dried cod, which no one on the prairies knew how to cook, was shipped from the Maritimes to feed the destitute. Apples and cheese, often not fit for human consumption, were shipped from Ontario. The Metis, of course, were affected along with everyone else; indeed, because they were poor going into the Dirty Thirties, they may have been hit even harder.

The devastation in the southern prairies increased the demand for land in northern Alberta, where many Metis had been squatting for years. Farm families moving from the south put pressure on the government to open more land for homesteading, and their demands ignited a conflict with the Metis squatters. The first confrontation occurred at Fishing Lake, near Cold Lake Alberta, where a number of Metis families had squatted on a forest reserve. Because of their experiences at St. Paul des Métis, they feared that they would once again be displaced and they had no desire to relocate again. As meetings were held to discuss the problem, talented leaders emerged and made the Metis cause a personal crusade. The most prominent were Malcolm Norris and Jim Brady.

Norris and Brady rank with the likes of Riel and Cuthbert Grant in the Metis' fight for recognition of their rights. Though their achievements attracted less public notice, in some ways they rank above those of Riel. Not only did they play an instrumental role in the establishment of Alberta's Metis settlements, they also helped revive Metis nationalism in Alberta and Saskatchewan. They were natural partners. Norris was a passionate orator, Brady a meticulous organizer. Both were avid readers and continued to study politics until their deaths. Unlike many of the Metis in Alberta, both came from well-to-do families.

Born in 1900, Norris was the son of John Norris, a wealthy Scot who made a fortune in the fur trade, and Euphrosine Plante, John's third wife. In spite of his wealth, John Norris regarded everyone — white, Indian or Metis — as his equal. But this did not stop him from doing a handsome trade in Metis scrip.

Malcolm Norris was a scholar. By the time he was an adult he spoke English, French and Cree. His father's death interrupted his plans for university, so Malcolm worked as a police officer with the North-West Mounted Police and a HBC trader before setting up his own trading business in northern Alberta. After a decade of fur trading he became interested in prospecting and to learn about the business he enrolled in geology courses at the University of Alberta. Malcolm Norris was one of the first prospectors in the Yellowknife area.

Brady also tried his hand at prospecting, but not until he moved to Saskatchewan in the late 1940s. His father, James Brady Sr., came from a wealthy Irish family. Inheritance money allowed him to study law in England, but a sense of wanderlust brought him to Canada. Eventually he settled in St. Paul des Métis, where he met and married Philomena Garneau, the first Metis nurse in Alberta and daughter of one of Louis Riel's supporters. Spending much of his time trying to help the Metis, Brady Sr. exposed the secret negotiations which had deprived the Metis of much of their lands in the St. Paul des Métis colony.

Given his background, it was not surprising that Jim Brady, born in 1908, should become a champion of the Metis cause. Rejecting formal schooling, he took up the career of an itinerant farm worker. However, while his co-workers indulged in drinking, billiards and dances, Jim spent his free time reading books on political theory, and was particularly fascinated by socialism. He later joined the Communist Party and also helped found the Lac La Biche local of the Co-operative Commonwealth Federation (CCF).

While Brady and Norris were important Alberta Metis leaders in the 1930s, there were others working for the cause who deserved recognition. Joe Dion, an enfranchised Indian (he voluntarily gave up his status under the Indian Act), worked as a teacher on the Keehewin Indian Reserve. A devout Catholic and a nephew of Big Bear, Dion admitted to having "a lively interest in the welfare of the Half Breeds." Pete Tompkins, an educated farmer-blacksmith, and Felix Calihoo, a St. Paul rancher, were also important figures in the rebirth of Metis nationalism in Alberta. The Metis Association of Alberta dedicated *Metis Land Rights in Alberta: A Political History*, to Brady, Norris, Dion, Tompkins and Calihoo.

Then there was Adrian Hope. Hope was born in 1903 of a Cree mother and an adventuresome Scottish father. His father was first a professor at a Scottish college, then a police officer in the NWMP and a soldier in the Boer War before trying farming in Alberta. Unsuccessful as a farmer, he took a job as an Indian agent. His son was just as restless; Adrian Hope's careers included rodeo-rider, film stuntman, ranch-hand and student. But his consuming passion was the Metis cause. He was to play many roles in support of the Metis, and he eventually became one of the founders of the Alberta Federation of Metis Settlement Associations.

The Metis Association of Alberta

The Fishing Lake Metis asked Joe Dion, by then a well-known local teacher, to help them. On May 24, 1930, Dion attended a meeting of some thirty Metis. He questioned whether any record was being kept of their meetings and was told that the people made a lot of speeches and then went home. Dion took charge and began to organize. He was asked to present the Metis case to government officials in Edmonton. He did not do so; instead, he arranged another meeting a month later to which he invited the local Member of the Legislative Assembly. At a meeting organized by Dion in 1931, over two hundred Metis decided to petition the provincial government — the United Farmers of Alberta (UFA) were then in power — for land and improved living conditions. Within a month, a five-hundred-name petition was presented to the Alberta government by Dion and the local MLA. The government listened but promised no action. The Metis met again in March 1932 and passed a resolution demanding land, this resolution, too, was sent to the government. Finally the government decided to act. It announced that a questionnaire was to be circulated among the Metis asking them about scrip, homesteading, the kind of machinery and livestock they owned and their views on farming. The government decided to let Dion and his supporters distribute and collect the questionnaires, a major victory for the fledgling Metis organization because it meant official recognition.

At the same time there was a move afoot to form a more formal Metis organization. It was at this stage that Brady, Norris and Hope became involved. The three helped organize a province-wide Metis convention, held on December 28, 1932, in St. Albert. The founding convention established L'Association des Metis d'Alberta et des Territoires du Nord Ouest, later to be known as the Metis Association of Alberta. Resolutions called for the establishment of Metis settlements with land to be held in the name of the Crown for the benefit of the Metis, the settlements envisaged were to be run by local councils, with the provincial association's executive council to be the supreme governing body of all settlements. Elected to the executive were Dion as president, Norris as first vice-president, Calihoo as second vice-president and Brady as secretary-treasurer. Within a year the association had 1,200 members in 41 locals — thanks to Brady and Norris who gave up months of their time to crisscross the province drumming up members.

The association's first priority was land. Brady set out a plan of action; they would start by petitioning the government, and if that failed they would go to the courts. As a last resort, they would work to elect members to the legislature who would be sympathetic to their cause.

Norris was successful in having Opposition MLAs raise the Metis question in the Alberta Legislature, with the result that in February 1933 the following motion was passed:

> Resolved that the Government should, during the next year, keeping particularly in mind, the health, education, relief and general welfare of the half-breed population, continue its study and enquiry into the problems and present its recommendations within ten days of the commencement of the next session thereof.

The government was in no hurry to meet the terms of the resolution. Finances were scarce in the Depression and much of Alberta's population was in dire straits. Alberta was also hoping that the federal government would assume responsibility for the Metis, in spite of the fact that the federal government refused any involvement.

In the fall of 1933 Norris and Dion met with Acting Premier G. Hoadley, Mines and Lands Minister R.G. Reid and his deputy Mr. Harvie. At this meeting Harvie suggested setting aside reserves for the Metis to be used as farming colonies for destitute Metis. At the same time rumours of a royal commission circulated. In the winter of 1934 the legislature passed yet another resolution calling for a public inquiry into the Metis' situation. The government procrastinated. Matters were further complicated when Premier John Brownlee's sexual involvement with his secretary became a matter of public knowledge and litigation and led to his resignation. The government was in total disarray. Finally, on July 17, 1934, the government announced the establishment of a royal commission. The appointment of the commissioners was not made until December; they included Judge Albert Ewing, who acted as chairman; Dr. Edward Braithwaite and James Douglas, described in the appointment as a "gentleman."

The Settlement Idea Revived

The commission was based in Edmonton but also held hearings at ten centres where the Metis predominated. A large number of Catholic clergymen testified about conditions amongst the Metis. Much of the Metis position was presented by Norris, Brady and Hope. Norris tried to build a case for Metis self-government based on past promises made but not kept. To this Ewing replied, "I do not see much good in raking up any mistakes that were made, or at least what some people may think were mistakes, years ago." Norris and Brady argued that settlements should be set aside for the Metis, which would provide a land base over which the Metis could exercise their right of self-government. Hope stressed the importance of the land being held by the Crown for the benefit of the Metis in perpetuity. At one point he said, "we've had enough of negotiable scrip...to buy booze....What we are asking for is land we cannot sell, cannot mortgage, but land to which we can belong."

The commissioners were profoundly biased against the Metis. Their prejudices are shown in the following excerpts:

> Commissioner Douglas: What is your opinion regarding the value to the half-breed of giving him an education?

> Bishop Breynat: I don't think he should be given too much education. Too much is bad for some of them. He needs just a little help — I think just until they are 13 or 14 years old probably.

> Chairman Ewing: I agree with you there, too much would be a bad thing.

> Mr. Pennock (lawyer for the Metis): You were speaking of the Half-breed owning land. I suppose the great trouble with the Half-breed is, he is irresponsible.

> Bishop Guy: Yes, like his white brother, he loves money but he cannot keep it.

And so the testimony went. Self-government and comprehensive Metis land claims settlement were issues before their time. To the commission the half-breed was not the equal of whites, and this attitude was reflected in its February 1936 report.

The commission concluded that the Metis were a destitute lot incapable of managing their own affairs. It recommended a government-run welfare scheme designed to turn the Metis into farmers. As the report put it:

> ...your Commissioners are of opinion that some form of farm colonies is the most effective, and, ultimately, the cheapest method of dealing with the problem....Each head of a family should be allotted a parcel of land. The title to the land should remain perpetually in the Crown...The allotment of a parcel would be a privilege....no half-breed would be compelled to join the colony but if he did not join he could have no claim for public assistance...as the Metis were the original inhabitants of these great unsettled areas and are dependent on wild life and fish for their livelihood, they should be given the preference over non-residents in respect of fur, game and fish.

Details for implementation were left with the government. However, the commission recommended that the Metis colonies should be near a lake (for fishing), have sufficient timber (to build log cabins), and have agricultural land as well as room for expansion.

The recommendation that farming settlements be established was not revolutionary. The government had hinted at the establishment of such settlements before the hearings and the Metis had argued for the same thing. But beyond that, there was no common ground between the two sides. For the government and commission, the settlements were to be colonies run by the government for the purpose of turning destitute Metis into farmers. For the Metis, the settlements were the land base on which they could practise self-government. This difference in perception blighted settlement-government relationships for decades and is still at the heart of the controversy today.

There was one obvious omission in the 1936 report. There is no evidence to indicate that it reviewed the operation of the St. Paul des Métis colony to determine the strengths and weaknesses of that experiment. Had it done so, the commission might have recognized that its recommendations were not likely to improve dramatically the lot of the Metis. Its recommendation of a cheap dictatorial welfare scheme was exactly the experiment that had failed at St. Paul des Métis.

The UFA government which appointed the commission lost every seat in the August 1935 election and was replaced by Canada's first Social Credit government. The new government decided to implement the commission's recommendations. The Metis Population Betterment Act (its name was later changed to The Metis Betterment Act) was passed in 1938 and stated in its preamble that the commission's recommendations should be given effect "by means of conferences and negotiations between the Government of the Province and representatives of the Metis population of the Province..." Reality was different. From the start, the government left no doubt that it was going to create the colonies and run them.

It was government legislation, and not the groundrules established by the Metis, which defined who could live on the colonies. At first, residence was restricted to those Metis "who are unable to secure out of their own resources a reasonable standard of living," but that provision was later dropped. A 1940 amendment defined "Metis" as someone who had at least one-quarter Indian blood. By this definition Louis Riel and probably Malcolm Norris and Jim Brady would not have qualified. The 1940 amendment was the first and only Canadian law that defined who was Metis.

By the fall of 1938 Tompkins and Dion had been hired by the government to locate sites for the colonies. Four sites were selected and approved by Christmas 1938. The Department of Health and its Bureau of Relief drafted regulations for the administration of the colonies. In this they were assisted by Dion and Tompkins, but by and large there was little consultation with the Metis. As a token, the government established a four-man Metis Committee which included Frank Buck as chairman, Dion, Tompkins and Dr. Braithwaite, a member of the Ewing Commission. The responsibilities of this committee were to assist the government in implementing the settlement scheme; its political purpose was to give the government credibility by allowing it to say that it did have input from the people most affected.

By 1940 eight colonies had been set up. Those in the Peace River area prospered, thanks to fishing, highway construction and plenty of good farm land. Those in the northeast (including what is today Kikino) were dependent on hunting, fishing and government relief. They were situated on poor farmland, and even today are much less prosperous than the Peace River settlements.

Authority over the colonies was left in government hands with the settlement residents having at most an advisory role. Three-man (later expanded to five-man) advisory boards were elected from the settlement, but they could do no more than offer their recommendations. A 1952 amendment required that the chairman be the government-appointed local supervisor of the settlement and that two of the remaining four members also be appointed by the government. Much to the disappointment of Metis leaders, the government's legislation and actions made it clear that there was no place for the Metis Association of Alberta in the administration of the settlements.

A 1943 cabinet order created a Metis Population Betterment Trust Account; legislation in 1979 converted it into the Metis Settlements Trust Fund. The fund, administered by the provincial cabinet minister in charge of the settlements (originally the Minister of Welfare — today the Minister of Municipal Affairs), was to be used for "the advancement and betterment of the members of Settlement Associations."

Metis families moving to the colonies were allotted land for farming plus one acre in the townsite. The land belonged to the Crown; occupants were given certificates of occupation which were theirs for life and which they could pass on to their heirs as long as they complied with the appropriate regulations.

Problems

The Ewing Commission had concluded in its report:

> ...we assume that the problem cannot be properly or adequately met by giving temporary assistance to individuals as the occasion seems to require. If met at all, the problem must be met by a comprehensive

scheme which will go to its root and offer an ultimate solution....We think, however, that over a long period of time the tendency will be to make the half-breed more and more dependent on farming and stock raising. This is the aim and purpose of the plan.

Did the government achieve its objective? There is no conclusive answer. What is clear is that the scheme suffered from excessive control by government and by a lack of locally controlled resources for economic development. It is telling that for many years the scheme was run by the Alberta Social Services Department.

The settlements were operated in a very paternalistic manner. There were many similarities to the way the federal Indian Act was used to control Indians and their reserves. Many decisions affecting a settlement were made by the settlement supervisor (a position somewhat akin to an Indian Agent on a Reserve). In 1941 Jim Brady took the job of supervisor of the Wolf Lake Colony. Often the same individual acted as supervisor of more than one colony. Pete Tompkins acted as supervisor in three colonies at the same time during the early 1940s. Sometimes the supervisor had another position — often teachers in the colony acted as the supervisors — and in the case of Kikino a medical doctor, who testified before the Ewing Commission, served as the first supervisor. Decisions on budgets, road construction, building and land allotment were all made by the supervisor. The supervisor was in turn responsible to the Metis Rehabilitation Branch (its name was later changed to the Metis Development Branch) in Edmonton. Legislation defined the role of the advisory board of the settlement as being to:

> ...co-operate with the Minister in preparing and for-
> mulating schemes (a) for the betterment of the
> members of the settlement association, and (b) for the
> settlement of members of the settlement association
> on lands of the Province set aside for the purpose.

There was no requirement for the minister to follow the
recommendations of the board, the majority of whose
members were appointed by him anyway. The minister,
through his agents, had absolute control over the settlements. Even if there was a dispute as to who was a Metis
the minister had the right to make the final decision, from
which there was no appeal.

The degree of control the government had was illustrated by the 1960 closure of the Wolf Lake Colony. In
spite of protests from the twelve families who lived in the
colony, it was closed by government order-in-council
(legislation governing the settlements has always given
cabinet the power to decide if land was no longer needed
for a Metis settlement). Residents were moved to other
colonies, an action the government justified on the
grounds that services could be better provided to these
families if they were moved to a more populous colony —
the same kind of reasoning the federal government used
to relocate Inuit families in the 1950s. The fact that the
settlement bordered the newly planned Primrose Lake
Air Weapons Range may have also influenced the decision.

Besides Wolf Lake, three other settlements were unilat-
erally dissolved between 1940 and 1960, including
Touchwood/Siebert in 1940, Marlboro in 1941 and Cold
Lake in 1960. The first two were dissolved shortly after

they were established, because too much land in these settlements had already been reserved for other purposes. Cold Lake was uninhabited at the time of its closure.

Excessive government control was not the only problem facing the colonies. In the four eastern colonies, the land was largely unsuitable for farming. "Much of the land in the Eastern Settlements...is unfit for good grain production," a 1972 government study concluded. In addition, there were provisions in The Metis Population Betterment Act which made agricultural development difficult. As in the Indian Act, property on a settlement was exempt from seizure by court order, and from all liens, charges and mortgages. This made it difficult for settlement residents to obtain financing for agriculture or other economic development. Before lending money financial institutions want security — a mortgage on land or liens against movable property. The 1972 government study concluded, "no alternative source of capital has ever been arranged for the Settlements to replace the mortgage system." Today, the settlements have formed their own settlement investment fund.

Another problem was that many Metis who were in need of assistance never benefitted from the scheme — today less than 10 per cent of Alberta's Metis population live on the settlements. In *The One-And-A-Half Men* author Murray Dobbin concluded, "...even indigent Metis were not moving onto the colonies. The government's determination to cut costs made any prospect of 'betterment' on the colonies remote. The government refused to provide transportation to the colonies."

The 1972 government study was just as critical, noting that the betterment scheme was not bettering anyone. Its major recommendation called for "extensive negotiations on specific issues between Government and the Settlement people with the object of establishing a relatively autonomous form of self-government in the Settlements."

It took thirteen years for that process to get underway. Before it did a major legal battle over oil and gas revenues intervened.

While settlements have received monies from oil companies for entry to their lands and surface rights, they have not received any compensation for the actual oil and gas. Indeed there is considerable legal uncertainty as to whether settlement lands include oil and gas. The cabinet orders creating the settlements stated that the settlements "...shall be entitled to surface rights only, until Regulations governing the administration of the various colonies have been approved." In examining the above provision in his study, *Subjugation, Self-Management, and Self-Government of Aboriginal Resources*, law professor Richard Bartlett concluded that it was "unsettled if the mineral rights were included in the areas set aside."

In 1969 the settlements sued the government for a court declaration that the latter had wrongly deposited some $6 million from the sale of oil and gas on settlement lands into the provincial treasury instead of the Metis Betterment Trust Fund. The lawsuit was dismissed on a procedural point. The court held that the Metis were wrong in suing the attorney-general; they should have sued the Minister of Welfare, the person in charge of the settlements.

Legal action was renewed in 1974 and today the lawsuit is still pending with an estimated $100 million at stake. In preparation for the case in June 1979 staff from the Social Services Department, on instructions from Crown counsel, raided six settlement offices and seized files pertaining to the lawsuit. Settlement office clerks were told that the files were being taken for audit. Settlement representatives maintain that some materials were missing from the files when they were eventually returned.

A complaint was made to the Alberta ombudsman by the president of the Alberta Federation of Metis Settlement Associations. The ombudsman concluded that, while the government had a right to look at the files (all settlement property is Crown property), the manner in which it exercised its right was regrettable and morally wrong. He suggested that the files could have been reviewed in settlement offices in the presence of settlement clerks. Besides recommending that the department should apologize to the settlements, he called for a change in the government-settlement relationship with a view to establishing self-rule for the settlements. He also called for a quick resolution of the litigation over oil and gas revenues (at the time of writing it was still pending and was still in the pre-trial stage).

Two events followed the ombudsman's report. Responsibility for the settlements was transferred from Social Services to the Department of Municipal Affairs. As well, in 1982 the Conservative government of Peter Lougheed established a committee — chaired by former lieutenant-governor Grant MacEwan — to review the Metis Betterment Act. The five-member committee included two representatives from the settlements and in its 1984 report was unanimous in its recommendations. Its principal recommendations called for granting title to settlement lands to the settlements themselves and allowing the settlements a greater measure of self-government.

Recent Events

The Lougheed government responded to the MacEwan report on June 3, 1985, when the Alberta Legislature unanimously passed a resolution calling for the transfer of ownership of settlement lands from the government to the settlements themselves and for constitutional protection for the lands so transferred. This protection was to be by an amendment to the Alberta Act, passed by Parliament in 1905 to create the Province of Alberta and which today serves as the province's constitution. The resolution also proposed a measure of self-government for the settlements and called upon the Metis to draft membership rules and to define the governing structure they wanted.

That Peter Lougheed should propose a measure of self-government and constitutional protection for Metis lands came as a surprise to more than one native rights advocate; after all, in the constitutional negotiations of 1981 Lougheed was a hardline opponent of greater recognition of native rights, and at the 1984 and 1985 constitutional conferences on aboriginal rights he strongly opposed entrenching self-government in the federal constitution. His motives for being generous to the Metis could have been many. Perhaps he simply wanted to show that Alberta could in fact devise a "made in Alberta" solution for dealing with aboriginal rights. Maybe he realized that the self-government he was proposing was still a conservative measure — like a municipal government, it would still come under the ultimate control of the provincial government. Perhaps at the end of his political career Lougheed wanted to do something in memory of his Metis grandmother Isabella Hardisty, or perhaps he wanted to do something to remove the taint from his grandfather's career. In his biography of Peter Lougheed, author Alan Hustak talked of Senator James Alexander Lougheed's wealth:

> There is some suspicion that not all of his wealth was earned legitimately. In order to deal with unsettled claims of Alberta's Metis population the federal government issued scrip certificates for 160 acres of land. Many of the Metis recipients of the scrip were persuaded by unscrupulous entrepreneurs to surrender their certificates for as little as a bottle of whiskey.

The illegal practice reached scandalous proportions and when a number of prominent Albertans faced prosecution for scrip fraud, Lougheed originated a bill in the Senate which imposed a three year statute of limitations on any such charges. In doing so he clearly protected a number of reputed millionaires, the foundation of whose wealth was built on fraud committed versus the Metis.

Even though the proposal covered only a small part of Alberta's Metis population — 4,000 out of an estimated 60,000 — Premier Peter Lougheed emphasized its importance:

> It doesn't overstate the motion to say that it's historic or to say it's unique; but perhaps even more impor-

tantly, it's a reflection of our judgement of the views of the majority of the citizens towards fair and equitable action for a minority within this province....I, personally, have hoped we could come to an approach which was pragmatic and fair but still was a step forward for the citizens of our province who live on Metis settlements.

Lougheed then spelled out his offer. The government would transfer title to lands occupied by Metis settlements to settlement associations. The ownership of minerals, however, was to remain with the provincial government — Alberta homesteaders never got mineral rights, why should the Metis? New provincial legislation granting the settlements self-governing powers would be passed. But first the Metis were invited to outline their views about who could be a settlement resident and about the type of governing institutions there should be on the settlements. Lougheed made clear that before the government started drafting legislation he wanted input from the Metis. Finally, the Alberta Act was to be changed so that Metis settlement lands could never be taken without the consent of the Metis themselves. The change to the Alberta Act would have to be approved by Ottawa as well, to ensure that it was constitutionally entrenched.

The Metis responded to the offer. In August, 1986 they presented a position paper to Premier Don Getty, Lougheed's successor, outlining how Metis government would work in the settlements. They too spoke of being at a "historic juncture." Their paper, entitled "By Means of Conferences and Negotiations We Ensure Our Rights," proposed two levels of government: a council for each settlement and a provincial governing body called a Metis Settlement Okimawiwin (Cree for "group of leaders"). In their proposal, settlement councils were given similar powers to a municipal government; the Okimawiwin was to have power over land-use policies, hunting and trapping policies, health, education and membership procedures in all the colonies. An appointed Elders committee would hear appeals from council decisions regarding land use or membership. If the elders committee could not decide, the applicant was given the right to apply to a Metis arbitration tribunal. The settlement council would decide who could be a member of the settlement in accordance with the guidelines established by the Okimawiwin.

In response to the Metis proposals the government released draft legislation in June, 1987, again inviting input from the Metis. The legislation adopted many of the ideas proposed by the Metis, but not all. In the matter of self-governing powers there are significant differences.

Under the proposed legislation the heavy hand of government will still be present in the administration of the settlements. The proposed new Metis Settlements Act gives settlement councils the same by-law-making and taxation powers that municipalities have. All by-laws have to be approved in a settlement vote and must conform with Okimawiwin policies. Settlements are also subject to various provincial laws, such as those dealing with traffic, liquor and surface rights for oil and gas exploration. By-laws which are in conflict with provincial legislation or Okimawiwin policy are void. Settlements are also prohibited from commercial activity or investing in securities except under ministerial regulation. The net effect is that economic development policies are subject to provincial censorship.

The Okimawiwin can make laws dealing with membership, land occupation, and hunting and trapping (in the last area, those laws can be made only in consultation with the minister in charge of native affairs). All Okimawiwin policies must be approved by 70 per cent of the settlements representing at least 70 per cent of all settlement residents. Okimawiwin policies can be vetoed by the minister (this is similar to the provisions of the Indian Act, which renders the by-law making powers of band councils subject to disallowance by the Minister of Indian Affairs).

A Metis Appeals Tribunal will deal with appeals pertaining to membership and land allocation. The tribunal can also mediate between settlement members, between a member and non-member, between settlements and between a settlement and the Okimawiwin. But its mediation role is limited to cases where both parties agree to mediation. The tribunal is not bound by rules of evidence and there is no requirement that its members be legally trained.

In essence, the Alberta scheme is one of delegation — the province is delegating some of its powers to the Okimawiwin and the settlements. Self-government is still one step away. Granting it will entail the creation of settlement bodies with exclusive authority in their areas of jurisdiction, in the way that provinces have the absolute right to make decisions regarding health, education and welfare.

The legislation gives the Metis settlements powers which they have not had before, though some of the devolution of power had started prior to the introduction of the draft legislation. The settlements will no longer be colonies. The provincial settlement association will be given an important role to play, something that the Metis have requested since the 1930s. If these changes work successfully, they could well be the stepping-stone from which the settlements can ask for greater powers in the future.

In theory, the new legislation applies to all Metis in Alberta. Anyone of aboriginal ancestry who identifies with Metis culture and history and can prove these facts either through genealogical records or sworn statements by Metis elders qualifies to live on the settlements. But there is a proviso — applications can be deferred if there is a lack of housing. The fact that all Metis can apply for membership gives the government the opportunity to argue that it has settled all Metis claims in Alberta, even though only a small minority of the province's Metis live on the settlements.

Government officials have indicated their intention to have the new scheme in place in 1988. There are still many differences to settle, and some parties to the discussions have expressed reservations about the government's ability to meet its timetable. Some observers, who have asked not to be named, have also suggested that the government's draft legislation might be dropped. In its place they foresee general legislation expressing the desire to see greater self-government for the settlements, with the details to be left for the provincial cabinet to decide.

Are the Settlements a Model for Other Land Claim Agreements?

Various provincial governments have started discussions with their Metis populations. Those discussions are at various preliminary stages. In all provinces the Metis' goal is to obtain a land base and the right to self-government on that land base. In Saskatchewan, land near Lebret (originally a Metis farm run by the Catholic Church) has already been transferred to a Metis non-profit corporation.

Much can be learned from the Alberta experience. In 1935 the Alberta Metis went into the Ewing Commission hearings looking for a land base. The government was looking for a cheap way to deal with destitute Metis. That difference in goals led to a system which both sides found unsatisfactory. Because the Alberta scheme was in essence a welfare measure, the government believed that it had to have significant control over the settlements. Today, that has proven to be unacceptable to the Metis, and the government itself has admitted that what was intended as a temporary measure ended up as something permanent.

The lesson to be gleaned from all of this is that welfare-type schemes have a tendency to perpetuate themselves. They also turn the people they are designed to help into powerless dependents. As Alberta has learned, a better route is to provide a secure land base on which communities can support themselves. This is not to suggest that the Alberta plan of 1987 is the final answer — it still falls short of true self-government. However, a careful study of the Alberta experiment can lead to the development of plans in other provinces which will recognize the Metis right to self-government without threatening provincial autonomy.

7
The Rebirth of the Metis

In 1885 the Metis had taken up arms in their quest for justice, and the government had responded with military force. Nearly one hundred years later, on April 16, 1984, the 350 Metis of Camperville, Manitoba (some four hundred kilometres north of Winnipeg), declared themselves an independent nation. They flew their own flag and declared absolute jurisdiction over education, justice, policing and over all game animals in a territory covering some five hundred square kilometres. This time the Canadian government sent no army; it simply ignored the Metis of Camperville. And after a day or two so did the media.

What had changed in one hundred years?

Governments have become more sensitive to native issues and now regard negotiation, not force, as the best way to respond to native demands. Coupled with that, the last three decades have seen the rise of a greater public awareness of native concerns. Overt talk of assimilating the natives has given way to accommodating them in the Canadian multicultural mosaic. Still, while there is a greater sensitivity on the part of governments and the public to native issues in Canada, the resolve to deal with them satisfactorily is lacking. Native issues are still not high in the priorities of most Canadians.

Changes in public attitudes are in part the result of the political and cultural resurgence of the Metis themselves. During the late 1960s and early 1970s Canada's native people engaged in protest and civil disobedience in order to force governments to come to terms with their grievances and demands. Native organizations proliferated across the country and played a key role in fighting for native rights. Political organization in native communities received a boost in the 1960s when the federal government began a policy of making grants to native organizations — whether this was to assuage guilt or to buy off the native radicals is a matter for debate. The Metis now had the benefit of experienced political activists while organizations such as the Indian-Metis Friendship Centres, and later the Gabriel Dumont Institute, worked to heighten the Metis' cultural awareness.

The end result was that in the constitutional negotiations of the late 1970s and 1980s the Metis — well organized politically and with a new-found pride in their cultural heritage — were in a strong position to make their case. And they succeeded. One of their greatest successes was having themselves defined as an aboriginal people in Canada's Constitution.

Political Organizations

There are many people who deserve credit for putting Metis issues on Canada's political agenda. Jim Brady and Malcolm Norris helped revive the Metis movement in Alberta in the 1930s, and in the 1960s they worked in

Saskatchewan to awaken Metis political consciousness there. Dr. Adam Cuthand was instrumental in organizing the Manitoba Metis Federation in 1967 and in 1968 was chosen as the first president of the National Metis Society, which in 1970 became the Native Council of Canada. Howard Adams, who served as president of the Metis Society of Saskatchewan from 1968 to 1970, fought vigorously for Metis rights until he moved to California in 1974 to accept a teaching position at the University of California. By that time, thanks to the efforts of Adams, Brady, Norris, Cuthand and many others, there were at least ten organizations representing Metis, including provincial organizations in B.C., Alberta, Saskatchewan, Manitoba, Ontario, Quebec and the N.W.T. The mandate of these organizations was to seek improved social conditions for the Metis, a land base and correction of historic grievances.

Of the Metis leaders of the 1960s and 1970s, Howard Adams stands out. Adams reflected the change in native leadership style that became evident in the early 1970s and is still prevalent today. That style included extensive use of the media, the threat of violence and the use of protests to capture public attention. Adams was well-suited for the new leadership style. Not only was he one of the first Metis to obtain a Ph.D., but more important he obtained his education at Berkeley in the turbulent early 1960s. In California he learned first-hand the techniques of radical militants, and on his return to Canada he applied those techniques in his work as a Metis activist. From the first, Adams' strident and militant oratory shocked Canadians out of their complacency. When he spoke, everyone, including the media, paid attention.

And it was the media's discovery of Adams that put him and the Metis cause in the national spotlight. The national media's love affair with Adams began at a federally funded workshop on native people held in Prince Albert, Saskatchewan, in 1967. There were many speakers at the workshop, including Malcolm Norris, but it was Adams' oratory and his threat of future violence — he said someday native people might have to pack guns like the Black Panthers — which captured the attention of the CBC.

Adams realized that if the media noticed, so would the general public. Until that time Canadians had ignored the Metis, even more than they did Indian people, indeed, there was a general assumption that the Metis' problems had been solved in 1885. Confrontational tactics and threats of violence, Adams believed, were necessary to convince Canadians that social and economic conditions among the Metis were desperate. The same strategies were necessary to awaken people to the fact that Metis demands were not simply part of the Indian problem — that the Metis were a unique people and had problems of their own. In spreading this message, Adams never minced his words. He told the federal Task Force on Poverty in 1969 that "Metis are developing a political consciousness of their wretched plight — the white supremacy [of] Canadian society. We have realized that we are at the bottom and have little or nothing to lose." Those comments made national news.

Yet there was more to Adams than inflammatory rhetoric — he was an organizer. He travelled the province and the country extensively. Some people still talk about Adams "charging around northern Saskatchewan in his

Volkswagen". He is also credited with alerting the Metis to the importance of speaking with one voice.

Adams was also a man of action. In 1968 Adams formed a native committee, called Saskatchewan's Native Action Committee, to run candidates in federal and provincial elections, and the committee ran its first candidate in the federal election that year. The committee also declared its intention to form a "provisional government" for the poverty-stricken Metis community of Green Lake in northern Saskatchewan. The rationale was to create a mechanism to deal directly with Regina and Ottawa and bypass the myriad layers of bureaucracy. Such activities led the Saskatoon *Star-Phoenix* to ask in an editorial: "Second Riel — or noisy illusion?"

In early 1970, as president of the Metis Society of Saskatchewan, he brought to public attention the plight of some nine hundred starving Metis in northern Saskatchewan. Politicians accused him of using the media to sensationalize a non-existent problem, but his tactics worked. The federal government carried out an investigation. The four-person investigating committee, composed of two members of Parliament, a senior civil servant and a political aide to federal Health and Welfare Minister John Munro, found no outright starvation. They did report, however, "shocking and disturbing squalor and living conditions." The Saskatchewan government promised housing assistance and Saskatchewan farmers, through a local branch of the National Farmers Union, donated twelve thousand pounds of flour to northern Metis communities.

Adams also organized protests against racism. In the early 1970s he organized a demonstration in front of a

Saskatoon hotel because the day before it had refused to serve Indians and Metis in its beer parlour. This incident, among others, prompted the Saskatchewan government to revamp its human rights laws. Other protest demonstrations were organized against government hiring policies.

Adams was and remains a controversial figure in both Metis and non-Metis circles. He has been described as everything from a "table thumper" to a "modern Grey Owl" and a "man ahead of his times". Perhaps the ultimate compliment came from the arch-conservative Saskatchewan premier Ross Thatcher when he offered Adams the position of deputy minister of the newly formed Department of Indian and Metis Affairs in 1969. Adams refused.

Of course, Adams' activities have to be seen in the context of the late 1960s and early 1970s, when marches and demonstrations against the Vietnam war, university administrations and multinational corporations were everyday occurrences. In the United States, blacks resorted to sit-ins, marches and violence in their struggle for equality. In Canada, Indian people occupied Indian Affairs offices and blocked roads and bridges. And in the midst of it all Trudeau rose to power on the promise of a just society.

Howard Adams helped lay the groundwork for future political action. Later, the growth of Metis organizations and of a new generation of leaders enabled the Metis to press for self-government, greater control over social services and for constitutional recognition. There would be no looking back.

Cultural Organizations

Parallel to the rise of Metis political organizations was the growth of organizations designed to provide support services to native people. Most notable among such organizations are the Indian-Metis Friendship Centres (often simply called Friendship Centres). From one centre in Winnipeg in 1959 the number of centres across Canada has grown to 108. Initially, the first centres were organized largely through the efforts of concerned non-natives. Today the centres are managed by all-native boards. While there is a National Association of Friendship Centres, each centre is locally run and controlled. In 1973 the federal government started a policy of funding Friendship Centres with annual operating grants made to each centre.

The centres are unique in that they serve both Indians and Metis and are primarily aimed at the urban native. The range of services available varies from centre to centre but includes recreational facilities, organized sporting events, bingo, dances, amateur talent contests, language classes, and craft and cultural classes. Often Alcoholics Anonymous groups operate from the centres, as do native courtworkers (courtworkers attend court and assist native people in understanding the charges and procedure and, if necessary, act as interpreters). Many centres have staff to assist the urban native in finding housing and employment. Sometimes, economic development schemes for native businesses are associated with the centres.

The centres are designed to provide native people with

an alternative to living on the street. They represent native self-government working at the community level. Sixty-eight-year-old Delia Gray described to the Edmonton-based native newspaper *Windspeaker* what the Edmonton Centre meant to her:

> This is a place I cannot leave. It's a place where people come for help, friendship, dancing and singing. This is the only place I can come speak Cree at. My husband passed away and my children don't speak Cree, so I have no one to converse with. But I come to the centre for that.

For status Indians, the reserve is the focal point of their Indianness. Even if they have left the reserve, they can still return to it for cultural and spiritual renewal. For the Metis, however, there are few places where they can go to renew their Metisism. In a sense the Friendship Centres play that role. And for many Metis people the centres have been places where they can develop and exercise management and administration skills, both of which will be needed if Metis self-government is to become reality.

There are, of course, other social service organizations besides the Friendship Centres. In the educational field there is the Gabriel Dumont Institute of Native Studies and Applied Research. The Regina-based Institute is the educational arm of the Association of Metis and Non-Status Indians of Saskatchewan. Since 1980 the Institute, through various distance-education programmes, has offered a variety of services to Saskatchewan's Metis people. Classes offered include university-level teacher training and employment training. Six years after its opening, it was serving 350 students and had graduated 146 students.

Curriculum research for a native education program reaching from kindergarten to grade twelve is one of the Institute's top priorities. It seeks to develop a separate school system for native communities in the same way that a Catholic school system has been established in many provinces. It has also developed curriculum materials for non-native schools in order to make students more aware of native history.

Along with educational activities the Institute employs researchers working on Metis rights questions. One result of this research was the 1985 book *1885: Metis Rebellion or Government Conspiracy?*, written by Don McLean and published by Pemmican Publications, a Winnipeg-based and Metis-controlled company. The Institute has also collected extensive material on scrip distribution. And it is carrying out research on Michif.

Of course, there are many other Metis institutions and organizations playing an equally important role in preserving and developing Metis culture. And the last few years have also seen the growth of Metis-controlled organizations whose goal is to promote economic development among the Metis. Such organizations have included the N.W.T. Metis Development Corporation Ltd., The Metis Economic Development Foundation of Saskatchewan and Sasknative Economic Development Corporation.

The 1982 Constitution

Over the 1960s and 1970s the Metis came to the conclusion that constitutional change was needed both to protect their culture and way of life, and to secure a land base and the right to self-government. Their views on the need for constitutional reform happened to coincide with Pierre Trudeau's belief that Canada needed a new constitution.

Discussions about constitutional reform began in 1927, but it was fifty-five years before those discussions led to fruition. Much of the activity was concentrated in the six years prior to 1982.

Early in 1976 Trudeau wrote to all the premiers asking them to join in repatriating the Constitution. Little came of this initiative. So in 1978 the Trudeau government introduced a white paper proposing a new Constitution, and then followed it with a bill. In the bill, native rights based on the Royal Proclamation of 1763 were immune from being overridden by a proposed Charter of Rights. The Royal Proclamation reserved undiscovered lands as Indian hunting grounds and further provided that Indian hunting grounds required for settlement had to be purchased by the Crown. Obviously, the bill offered little to the Metis. The bill was Trudeau's way of forcing action in constitutional reform, but it was allowed to die as other events took over.

Throughout 1978 and 1979 the three national native groups — The National Indian Brotherhood (now known as the Assembly of First Nations), The Native Council of Canada and the Inuit Tapirisat — lobbied for additional constitutional protection. At the October 1978 conference these groups were granted observer status, and at the next conference in February 1979 the ministers agreed that future discussions would include the topic of "Canada's Native People and the Constitution."

Constitutional reform continued during Joe Clark's brief prime ministership, though it was not the government's chief priority. Native people won an important concession from Clark at the December 3, 1979, ministerial conference on the Constitution: they were allowed to speak — rather than merely observe — on issues affecting native people. When Trudeau returned to power in February 1980 the Constitution once again became one of the central issues of national politics. Indeed, after Quebecers rejected sovereignty-association in the referendum of May 1980, Trudeau's commitment to constitutional renewal became stronger than ever. Impatient with the lack of progress in the constitutional talks, and anxious to assure Quebecers that there was a place for them in Confederation, Trudeau announced on October 2 that the federal government would make a unilateral request to the British Parliament. Shortly afterwards the government submitted its constitutional resolution to Parliament. This resolution made provision for a Charter of Rights but offered no protection for aboriginal rights. Trudeau attributed this omission to the difficulty in defining aboriginal rights.

By the fall of 1980, native groups had been fairly successful in obtaining public support for their efforts to entrench natives rights in the Constitution — The Canadian Bar Association, the Robarts-Pepin Task Force on National Unity, a Joint Senate-House of Commons Committee on the Constitution, the Primate of the Anglican Church and the Ontario Conference of Catholic Bishops all called for special provisions in the Constitution protecting native rights. However, after the Trudeau government introduced its resolution in October 1980, the lobbying campaign achieved a new level of intensity. Native groups besieged the Canadian and British Parliaments as well as the United Nations, urging those bodies to lend their weight in pressuring the Canadian government to protect native rights in the Constitution.

The lobbying worked. On January 30, 1981, Minister of Justice Jean Chrétien introduced an amendment to the proposed Constitution which "recognized and affirmed" the "aboriginal and treaty rights" of Canada's aboriginal people. Aboriginal people were defined to include the Indian, Inuit and Metis people. The amendment also mentioned that a conference would be held within two years to define aboriginal rights, and aboriginal representatives would be invited.

The initial reaction of native leaders was described by Roy Romanow in 1983 (he was Saskatchewan's attorney-general during the constitutional talks).

> In response to public pressure, the federal government suddenly and dramatically reversed itself on the question of entrenching aboriginal rights in the constitution. The government proposed an amendment that would give positive recognition to treaty and aboriginal rights. This was followed by a remarkable about-face by aboriginal leaders. Some now said...they would join the federal government in urging the British government to approve the

constitution resolution despite the objections of the
provinces.

But the harmony was short-lived. Soon a group of Alberta
Indian chiefs were petitioning the Queen and British
Parliament to refrain from patriating the Constitution
until all Indian claims were met. They also started a court
action seeking a declaration that England was responsible
for all treaties. The English courts rejected their claim.

To placate the provinces, in the spring of 1981 the
federal government referred its constitutional bill to the
Supreme Court of Canada. On September 28, in a seven
to two decision, the court ruled in Ottawa's favour;
however, six judges stated that, according to constitutional convention, the resolution should have "substantial" provincial approval.

A federal-provincial constitutional conference followed and on November 5, 1981, Ottawa and all provinces, except Quebec, agreed on a new Constitution. That
draft constitution dropped all protection for native rights.
Chrétien later explained in his book *Straight from the
Heart*: "To get the consent of the majority of the provinces, the federal government had...to drop aboriginal
rights from the charter." Roy Romanow, writing in *The
Quest for Justice*, had a slightly different recollection:

> The aboriginal peoples' London lobby confirmed in
> the minds of federal and provincial governments that
> the original section 34 [providing protection for
> aboriginal rights and treaties] should not be retained
> because it was contrary to the wishes of the Indian
> community. Of course, there were other factors. The

demand for entrenchment of aboriginal rights was not fully understood by many of the governments, and those who thought they understood it expressed reservations about its implications for provincial jurisdiction.

The deletion of protection for aboriginal and treaty rights produced an immediate public backlash from both native and non-native groups. Astonishingly, even a federal cabinet minister criticized the move. So did Thomas Berger, then a judge. His comments in a speech at Guelph and in a *Globe and Mail* editorial cost him his judgeship.

Within weeks the first ministers changed their position. Peter Lougheed was the last holdout and he agreed to include aboriginal rights in the draft constitution if the word "existing" was added. Section 35 of the Constitution now read: "The existing aboriginal and treaty rights of the aboriginal peoples of Canada are hereby recognized and affirmed." Aboriginal people were again defined to include the Indian, Inuit and Metis peoples.

The word "existing" was a red flag to native leaders. For them it meant that no new rights, such as self-government, could be acquired by native peoples and that only those rights existing when the Constitution came into force would be protected. They feared that rights which native people had enjoyed, but which had been taken away before 1982, would not be protected. (For example, most Indian treaties guaranteed the right to hunt game birds, but the Migratory Birds Convention Act, passed by Parliament in 1917, limited the season when Indians could hunt game birds.) To date, the court decisions have left considerable confusion on the meaning of the word "existing," with the consensus being that rights given up by Indians and Metis prior to the adoption of the new Constitution are not resurrected. Despite native protests, the draft constitution was passed by Parliament in December and was approved by the British Parliament several months later. The Queen came to Ottawa on April 17, 1982, to proclaim the Constitution in force from that day on.

Constitutional Protection for Metis Rights

That the Metis were mentioned in the Constitution was a matter of hard work. It did not happen by accident. The first drafts of the Constitution in 1978 and 1980 had spoken only of "native peoples of Canada" (which may or may not have included the Metis — because of their mixed blood origins some lawyers and political scientists have argued that the Metis are not native people). It was only in 1981 that the word "Metis" was first included in a draft of the constitution. The amendments presented by Jean Chrétien to the House of Commons on January 30, 1981, specifically mentioned the Metis for the first time. The effect of this amendment put beyond doubt the fact that the Metis were an aboriginal people and therefore that their aboriginal rights, if they were found to have any, would be protected.

Howard Leeson, a professor at the University of Regina who, during the late 1970s and early 1980s, was

Saskatchewan's deputy minister of Intergovernmental Affairs, suggests that it was Saskatchewan — after lobbying by the Metis — which first argued for mentioning the Metis specifically in the Constitution. However, at the 1987 constitutional conference Premier Getty of Alberta credited his province with helping to achieve this goal. "I recall with pride the role of Alberta in having the Metis included in the Constitution," he said.

Clem Chartier, a Metis National Council leader, tells another version. He says that in January 1981, Jean Chrétien called in the leaders of the Indian, Inuit and Metis people asking for their support for patriation of the Constitution in return for a constitutional guarantee of aboriginal and treaty rights. They agreed. The Native Council of Canada, which at the time represented the Metis, asked that the Constitution spell out who the aboriginal people were so as to ensure that it included the Metis. Chrétien accepted this proposal. All of this, according to Chartier, took place in a 15-minute meeting in the corridors of Parliament, while a parliamentary committee was examining a draft version of the new Constitution.

As we have seen, ten months later, in November 1981, in order to appease the provinces and get their support for a new constitution, the protection for treaty and aboriginal rights, along with the section defining the aboriginal people, was dropped from the draft constitution, only to be reinstated after a public outcry. The Metis were just as active as other native groups in insisting that the aboriginal clauses be reinserted, and they shared the victory.

Yet what had they gained? Are actual rights protected or is section 35 a hollow promise for the Metis? In the

1800s some Metis communities lived with Indian tribes, and many of those communities were allowed to join Indians in signing treaties. Clearly, section 35 protects those Metis rights. (However, under the current Indian Act those Metis are in fact considered status Indians.) But the majority of the Metis did not enter into treaties with the federal government. What does the Constitution offer them?

And it is here the problem lies. While the Constitution says that the Metis are aboriginal people it does not give them any aboriginal rights. It only protects those rights which they had at the time the Constitution came into force (April 17, 1982) and any rights they might gain under a future land claims or self-government agreement. Whether the Metis had aboriginal rights on April 17, 1982 is a question of considerable legal and historical debate.

A 1979 Federal Court of Canada decision set out four criteria which must be met to prove aboriginal title (one part of aboriginal rights). They are that the aboriginal people and their ancestors were members of an organized society, that that society occupied the territory which they claim, that they excluded all other people from occupation, and that occupation was an established fact by the time England asserted sovereignty.

Thomas Flanagan has argued strongly against Metis aboriginal rights. "There are many difficulties in categorizing the Metis as an aboriginal people," he said at a 1983 conference in Lethbridge. Commenting on the four criteria needed to prove aboriginal title, he said, "the Metis seem to be disqualified on all four counts." The Metis were never a distinct society, he argues, but part of the larger fur-trade society of whites and Indians. They had no exclusive territory; rather they roamed across the west and shared their land with the Indians and the whites. Finally, he argues that the Metis could not have occupied their territory at the time England asserted sovereignty because they are in fact a product of contact between Europeans and Indians.

The Metis reply that the federal government has specifically recognized the Metis' aboriginal rights. They point to section 31 of the 1870 Manitoba Act which gave the Metis 1.4 million acres "for the extinguishment of Indian Title." And they point to provisions such as the Dominions Lands Act of 1879 which gave the governor-in-council the power "to satisfy claims existing in connection with the extinguishment of the Indian title preferred by the half-breeds resident in the North-West Territories...." Because of fraud and government conspiracy, the Metis say, they never got the benefits they were supposed to receive. However, the federal government, having recognized the Indian title of the Metis in the 1800s, is now bound by its declarations. Their position, therefore, is that they do indeed have aboriginal rights and their aboriginal rights are protected by the Constitution.

The federal government disagrees. During the month of April 1981, then Justice Minister Jean Chrétien wrote to various provincial Metis organizations denying their claim for land rights. He stated that, even if the Metis had aboriginal rights, the federal government had settled with the Metis by the terms of the Manitoba Act and the scrip system established under the Dominion Lands Act in the 1880s. By and large, the government has maintained this position throughout the constitutional talks of the 1980s.

If, either through negotiation or by court decision, the

Metis are found to have land rights, who has to find the land or money to compensate the Metis for the land they lost? In view of mounting government deficits at both the provincial and federal levels, this is no small question.

Section 91(24) of the Constitution Act makes the federal government responsible for "Indians, and Lands reserved for Indians." The Metis have long argued that they are included in this section. They point to a 1939 Supreme Court of Canada decision which found that the federal government was responsible for providing social services for the Inuit of northern Quebec. If the Inuit fall within section 91(24), the Metis argue that they do as well. They note that the federal government has legislated to deal with the Metis in the past, citing provisions in the Manitoba Act and the Dominion Lands Act. Over the years, they observe, the federal government has funded various Metis activities. They point to the federal Secretary of State providing core funding for Metis organizations, for Indian and Metis Friendship Centres, for northern broadcasting, for native conferences and for land claims research by Metis organizations. The federal Department of Justice grants scholarships to Metis students to study law; funding for Metis housing programs comes from Canada Mortgage and Housing Corporation; and the Department of Small Business makes grants to all native businesses under the Special Agricultural and Rural Development Act. Most recently, the Metis National Council has received funding to participate in the last four constitutional conferences on aboriginal rights. As a result, the Metis take the position that the federal government, having committed itself to fund Metis activities and programmes, cannot now deny responsibility.

The MNC has pressed the federal government, without success, to refer to the Supreme Court the issue of whether section 91 (24) includes the Metis. Why do the Metis want to be a federal responsibility? All of Canada's native people feel the federal government has generally been more sympathetic to native issues than have the provinces. A recent example they point to is the refusal by Alberta and Saskatchewan to put self-government in the Constitution. Like many Canadians, the Metis feel the federal government is more likely to take a broad national view than a narrow parochial one.

The 1983 Constitutional Conference

The Constitution Act of 1982 required a constitutional conference be held within one year to identify and define aboriginal rights. That conference was held on March 15 and 16, 1983. Another three conferences followed between 1984 and 1987, but the 1983 conference was the only one that achieved significant progress.

Before the Metis could attend the 1983 conference they had to decide who would represent them. Since its formation in 1970, the Native Council of Canada had spoken nationally for the Metis. It, however, was composed of both Metis and non-status Indians — two groups whose agendas were fundamentally different. The non-status Indians wanted recognition as Indians and the same rights as status Indians had. The Metis had no desire to become Indians. They wanted recognition as a distinct aboriginal people. They also wanted the government to live up to commitments it had made under the Manitoba Act and under the scrip system. The Metis were also unhappy with the Native Council of Canada's definition of Metis — to the NCC, Metis means anyone of mixed blood origin regardless of where they live or whether their origins were in the Red River.

Invitations to the 1983 constitutional conference were at the sole discretion of the prime minister, and he invited the Native Council of Canada to represent the Metis. At a February 1983 meeting of federal-provincial officials the Metis asked for a separate seat at the constitutional conference. Their request was denied. They then split from the NCC and formed the Metis National Council (MNC); they also launched a court action in Ontario for an injunction blocking the conference from proceeding without Metis representation. Before the judge had an opportunity to rule on their request, Trudeau relented and invited the Metis National Council to take part in the conference.

At the 1983 conference there was an agreement that no constitutional changes affecting aboriginal rights would be made without a constitutional conference to which aboriginal people were invited. (This did not go as far as some aboriginal leaders had hoped — that is, an absolute veto over constitutional changes affecting them.) The parties also agreed that another constitutional conference would be held in 1984 and two more before April 1987. The agenda of the 1984 conference would include self-government, equality rights, treaties, aboriginal title and rights, and land and resources. Because the Metis do not have a land base, the last two issues were of particular importance to them.

Two other items were agreed upon. The constitutional

guarantee for existing treaty and aboriginal rights was extended to include future land claims agreements — a significant provision for the Metis since it would give constitutional protection to any land settlement that might be successfully negotiated in future. And the Constitution was amended to guarantee sexual equality in the area of constitutionally protected aboriginal and treaty rights. The sexual-equality amendment created some difficulty. While there was agreement in principle on aboriginal rights applying equally to men and women, immediately after the conference the Inuit Tapirisat and the NCC insisted that the wording had been changed without their consent. This issue was to lead to considerable acrimony at the 1984 and 1985 conferences.

The 1984 and 1985 Conferences

Follow-up conferences were held on March 8 and 9, 1984 and April 2 and 3, 1985. A great deal of time was spent at both conferences arguing about the sexual-equality section. Unfortunately, the dispute hindered progress in other areas. The equality issue also gave rise to a debate on the subject of Metis rights. The NCC argued that the equality section should not only guarantee equality between the sexes but also equality between aboriginal groups. The government rejected the argument. If it had not, the Metis would have been in a good position to demand a land claims settlement, because the government has already recognized that Indians and Inuit have land rights.

The other major issue discussed at the two conferences was self-government. Between 1984 and 1985 a Liberal government had been replaced with a Conservative one, and yet the federal proposals on self-government were remarkably similar at both conferences. These proposals recognized the right of aboriginal people to self-governing institutions, and stated that the jurisdiction, powers, and financing of those institutions were to be negotiated with the provinces and the federal government. The 1985 proposal went one step further than the 1984 one in that it offered constitutional protection for any self-government agreements that were negotiated.

At the 1984 conference the federal proposal for self-government was strongly supported by Manitoba, Ontario and New Brunswick, but foundered on the opposition of B.C., Alberta and Saskatchewan and also of the native groups. The main concern of native groups was that the envisaged self-governing institutions would not be protected in the Constitution. They also feared that the negotiations about these institutions might never take place, or, alternatively, might drag on forever or bog down in a stalemate. They wanted something more concrete.

Some observers suggest that the expectations of the parties at the 1984 conference were not high. Just prior to the 1984 conference Trudeau had announced his resignation and no one expected him to initiate any bold new measures.

The 1985 conference began where the 1984 one had left off. This time, there were great expectations for the talks — Prime Minister Brian Mulroney, the great labour conciliator, was in the chair — and this conference indeed came close to an agreement. In the end, however, the process failed because of opposition from the two western provinces and two out of four native groups.

On the first day of the conference Saskatchewan, Alberta and B.C. refused to include a statement in the Constitution recognizing self-government until that principle was defined. On the second day Saskatchewan tried to break the impasse by proposing an amendment in which constitutional recognition of self-government was contingent upon negotiation (there was no commitment to negotiate in the proposal). It was accepted by six other provinces and the federal government; Alberta and British Columbia opposed it, while Quebec abstained since it refused to recognize the 1982 Constitution. Although there were sufficient votes to pass the amendment, the prime minister wanted the support of the aboriginal organizations. The MNC and the NCC decided to support the Saskatchewan formula after Mulroney agreed that he would meet with them to discuss a land base for the Metis and non-status Indians. The Assembly of First Nations, however, rejected the proposal because it contained no commitment that negotiations implementing the principle of self-government would be undertaken. The Inuit Tapirisat withheld their judgement for further consultation with their people.

The prime minister adjourned the conference until June 5 and 6, 1985, so senior cabinet ministers from all governments and aboriginal leaders could continue discussions and the Inuit could work out their position. The June meeting, however, came to nothing.

While the 1985 conference was generally a failure, the Metis did achieve a small victory. As already mentioned, in return for MNC and NCC support, Mulroney promised to discuss land claims with these groups. The following exchange took place.

> Brian Mulroney, Prime Minister of Canada:
> Both I and the federal government accept that the Metis and non-status people have unique problems regarding the protection of their rights. I, of course, confirm today — as I have in other circumstances — a commitment to recognize their special needs. I am going to be convening a meeting which I will personally chair with the leaders of the Metis and non-status people, with Mr. Crombie and Mr. Crosbie, to examine ways in which we can work together to guarantee their rights and obtain that equality which the Constitution Act envisaged. It is somewhat overdue.

> Harry Daniels, Native Council of Canada:
> Thank you Mr. Prime Minister. I have one question for you only before I make my statement. Just prior to coffee break you made a statement vis-à-vis your willingness to set up a bilateral process or some talks with the Metis and non-status Indians with regard to our unique rights and our special needs. Did that include the discussion on a need for a land base for our people?

> Prime Minister Mulroney: Yes.

The promised meeting never took place. Nevertheless, the above exchange represented the first public acknowledgement by the federal government that it had some responsibility for the Metis.

The 1987 Conference

Of the four constitutional conferences on aboriginal rights, the 1987 one was the greatest disaster. In contrast to previous conferences, the whole of the first day was taken up with opening statements. There was no negotiation. Many participants left the impression that they were simply filling in time with their long-winded speeches in order to fulfil the constitutional requirement that another conference be held. All of the parties stressed the need for aboriginal people to have greater control over their daily affairs, but they could not agree on what words should be put in the Constitution or whether the Constitution should make any reference to self-government.

Provinces opposing self-government spent considerable time placing their position in the best light.

Premier Grant Devine pointed out that Saskatchewan's 1985 proposal almost became law and noted that his government was working to resolve treaty land entitlement issues and was discussing land transfers with the Metis. He argued that most Canadians did not understand what self-government meant. Finally, he argued that, while polls revealed the majority of Canadians to be in favour of self-government, they also indicated that 77 per cent of Canadians saw assimilation as the answer.

Alberta premier Don Getty pointed out that his province was making considerable progress in granting self-government to its Metis settlements. He also claimed credit, on behalf of Alberta, for having the Metis included in the Constitution (a contention which was not universally accepted).

The premier of British Columbia, Bill Vander Zalm, who was often heckled by the native participants, talked about the Sechelt Band in B.C., which by federal and provincial agreement was given municipal-style self-government in 1986. He argued that the impact of self-government would not be equal on all provinces because 72 per cent of all Indian reserves in Canada were in British Columbia.

Newfoundland premier Brian Peckford, who had supported constitutional entrenchment of self-government in 1985, changed his position. "We are a welfare society," he told aboriginal leaders, "yet you look up to me because I have provincial status. I'm not sure if you're being as smart as you think you are." He then suggested that, if Newfoundland had to vote again on whether to join Canada, he was not sure what the result would be. His position may have been influenced by the recent signing, without Newfoundland's consultation, of the Franco-Canadian fishing accord.

The federal government did not present a proposal on the first day. Rather, federal officials worked through the night to prepare a position for the second day. Much of that day was spent in closed session but no progress resulted. Some aboriginal leaders alleged that the federal government had once again breached its "trust responsibility" to native people by not showing more leadership at the conference.

The aboriginal leaders were united at the conference. They all agreed beforehand on a common position, namely, that self-government was an inherent (meaning they always had it) right and that its implementation would be subject to negotiations in "good faith." Their proposal required governments to enter into self-government negotiations; it affirmed the inherent right of the Indian, Inuit and Metis people to a land base; and it gave aboriginal people the right, if they so chose, to call for treaty renegotiations. The aboriginal people did not move from their position during the two-day conference.

Yvon Dumont of the Manitoba Metis Federation, speaking on behalf of the Metis National Council, expressed his concern at the absence of Quebec premier Bourassa because "Quebec supported us in 1870 and 1885." In response to Dumont, Prime Minister Mulroney said, "by your very presence you remind us of an unhappy chapter in our history."

Louis "Smokey" Bruyere, from the Native Council of Canada, asked what had happened to the other agenda items agreed upon in 1983. All of the conferences since had focused on self-government and items such as "land and resources," which are extremely important to the Metis, were never discussed.

The conference ended in recriminations. Prime Minister Mulroney showed annoyance with some of the western provinces when he said, "we had seven provinces on side in 1985...some people have started to go backwards." The strongest attacks came from Jim Sinclair, a Metis National Council spokesperson and leader of the Saskatchewan Metis, who launched a verbal tirade against Premiers Vander Zalm and Devine. "By leaving here today without an agreement, we have signed a blank cheque for those who want to oppress us and hold racism against us," he said. He accused the Saskatchewan government of spending millions on jails to house natives but doing nothing to allow them to run their own affairs. He also accused it of subsidizing wine and whiskey in northern native communities, but not milk.

Turning his attention to Vander Zalm, Sinclair called him a hypocrite. Vander Zalm talked about Canadian native soldiers helping liberate his native Holland, Sinclair said, but now he would not grant those soldiers their freedom.

Why Failure?

After $50 million and five years the constitutional process ended without concrete results. On the positive side, the process gave native issues a public profile they had not had before, while also providing native leaders with political experience at the national level. On the negative side, hopes which had been raised in 1982 were brutally smashed.

Talks and discussions towards self-government will continue, albeit at a much slower pace. If present trends continue, those talks are likely to lead to municipal models of government rather than a third level of government with inherent jurisdiction independent of other levels of government. Without constitutional protection, native leaders fear that what is given one day could just as easily be taken away the next. And with no constitutional requirement for such talks to continue, the process will obviously be much slower.

The differences between what the aboriginal peoples want and what most governments are prepared to offer can be easily summed up. In the case of the aboriginal peoples, their position is that the Constitution should recognize their inherent right to self-government and require the provincial and federal governments to enter into negotiations to implement that right. This position is built on decades and indeed centuries of mistrust. The Metis, for example, look at the Manitoba Act, the scrip system and Mulroney's 1985 promise to discuss a land base, and feel betrayed. Consequently, they and other aboriginal groups argue for a concrete guarantee in the Constitution which can be enforced in the courts.

The position of most governments — even governments supportive of a constitutional amendment are reluctant to go as far as aboriginal leaders want — is to negotiate first, and then to protect in the Constitution any rights agreed on by such a process. Many governments also want the commitment to negotiate to be open-ended; in short, they see self-government as something they give to aboriginal peoples on the government's own timetable. Their fear is that, if an unqualified right to self-government is put in the Constitution and negotiations then fail, the courts may define self-government in a way that will prove to be unacceptable to them. Many provinces are also worried that aboriginal self-government might reduce their powers. Hence, they have argued that self-government, and more particularly its day-to-day workings, must be defined in detail before the principle can be constitutionalized.

Curiously, while some premiers have expressed a reluctance to put self-government into the Constitution until it is defined, they have put other undefined rights into the Constitution. The principle of equalization, for example, is enshrined in the Constitution. Section 36(2) provides:

> Parliament and the government of Canada are committed to the principle of making equalization payments to ensure that provincial governments have sufficient revenues to provide reasonably comparable levels of public services at reasonably comparable levels of taxation.

That clause is filled with unanswered questions, yet the premiers had no hesitation in putting it in the Constitution when it was being drafted in the early 1980s. Similarly, Canada's Charter of Rights is "subject...to such reasonable limits prescribed by law as can be demonstrably justified in a free and democratic society." Already this vaguely worded qualification has been the subject of considerable litigation.

At most, a constitution is a set of principles by which a society conducts its collective life. It is a guide for parliamentarians and the courts on the kind of society we are. It cannot be a detailed analysis of every possible event which one day may face society. Why, then, the reluctance on the part of many leaders to put aboriginal self-government in the Constitution? Perhaps the political will is still lacking. Canada's aboriginal people are not a large voting-block and in most Canadians' minds aboriginal issues are not high on the national agenda.

It is unfortunate, too, that the last three conferences concentrated solely on self-government. Land is an important issue to all native people, especially the Metis.

Perhaps if those other items listed in 1983 had been discussed, progress might have been achieved.

In 1982 a lot of expectations were raised, but five years later those expectations were left unfulfilled. Native people can point to this as yet another instance when they have been betrayed by Canada. Their situation can be compared to the plight of the starving man who sees people holding out bread in front of him. The man is allowed to touch and smell the bread; then just when it seems to him that he can have the bread, it is taken away. This is what has happened with native people. The constitutional conferences teased native people into believing that a new era of constitutional protection of their rights was at hand. But then their hopes were dashed. What was especially galling to native leaders was the speed with which the Meech Lake Accord was reached to accommodate Quebec's concerns about the Constitution.

The Meech Lake Accord

A month after the failed aboriginal constitutional conference Canada's first ministers reached an agreement to amend the Constitution to satisfy Quebec's aspirations. After the tedious negotiations on aboriginal rights, most Canadians were stunned at the speed with which the negotiations proceeded. On June 3, thirty-five days after the agreement in principle had been reached and after a marathon all-night session, Canada's first ministers produced the actual wording for the amended Constitution. It recognizes Quebec as a distinct society, and allows the provinces a say in immigration and in appointments to the Supreme Court of Canada and the Senate. Provinces are

given the right to opt out of future national social programmes and receive compensation from Ottawa. The
requirements governing amendment to the Constitution
were also changed. Under the prior constitution, Ottawa
and seven provinces with 50 per cent of the population
could make amendments. Under the Meech Lake Accord,
the consent of all provinces will be needed to effect
certain changes. These changes involve such things as
Senate reform, the role of the Queen, Governor-General
and Lieutenant-Governors, and the creation of new provinces.

To the Dene, Metis and Inuit of the Northwest Territories, the latter requirement could be a major setback. They
have been negotiating to divide the Territories into two
separate entities, with the hope that eventually these new
governments might become provinces. Given the Meech
Lake Accord's more onerous requirement for the creation
of new provinces, that goal may be more difficult to
achieve. Residents of the Northwest Territories and of the
Yukon also fear that the new provisions will prevent them
from having a say in appointments to the Senate and
Supreme Court of Canada. That privilege is reserved for
the provinces. Some people in the Territories purchased
full-page advertisements in several newspapers to make
their concerns known and have, along with people in the
Yukon, begun a court challenge to block the Accord from
becoming law.

The Accord makes only passing reference to Canada's
aboriginal people. In recognizing Quebec as a distinct
society, the Accord states that it will not affect any rights
native people already have under the Constitution.
Georges Erasmus, National Chief of the Assembly of

First Nations, was critical of this limited provision. Shortly after the accord was signed he stated:

> While the clause can almost be interpreted as a non-derogation clause, it does not go far enough in protecting our rights. It protects those rights in Section 2 of the accord but says nothing about the rest of the amendment. For instance, federal programs which Indian people rely on can be opted out of by the provinces, providing they conform to national objectives — this could lead to erosion of the trust responsibility the federal government has towards Indians....

The same can be said about the Metis. They receive some federal funding. Under the Accord, presumably, a province could opt out of a future social programme which provides funding for the Metis. For example, at a future date the provinces and Ottawa could sign an agreement on Metis education. Afterwards, it would be possible for a province to opt out as long as it provided an alternate service which met national objectives, in this case the education of the Metis. The provincial programme could in fact be inferior to that provided in the federal-provincial agreement, but the province would still receive federal funds.

The Accord does hold out a small hope for Canada's aboriginal people. It requires annual constitutional conferences to discuss senate reform, fisheries and "such other matters as are agreed upon." Those other matters could include continued discussions on aboriginal rights. However, the holding of such discussions would require the prior consent of Ottawa and all provinces.

At the time of writing the Accord was not yet law. It had been approved by the Quebec, Saskatchewan and Alberta legislatures and by the House of Commons. It has to be passed in the Senate and every provincial legislature before becoming law. A number of groups, aboriginal and non-aboriginal, have lobbied legislators to include a provision which not only recognizes Quebec as a distinct society but also recognizes aboriginal people as distinct societies with distinct rights. In addition the Accord has run into serious opposition on other grounds, including the failure to protect women's rights, the decentralization of power to the provinces, the difficulty in reforming the Senate after the Accord becomes law, and the power granted to provinces in regard to appointment of judges to the Supreme Court of Canada. The all-party parliamentary committee studying the Accord called, in its report, for the federal government to continue to fund native groups in preparing their constitutional case. It also called for a first ministers' conference on aboriginal rights to be held by April 17, 1990.

To Canada's native people the Accord showed that, when there is the political will, agreement can be achieved. Obviously, in the case of many of Canada's politicians, there was no will to accommodate the concept of self-government.

The Situation Today

The failure of the constitutional process has taken much of the fight out of many Metis political organizations. And they have suffered other blows, too — in many cases governments have cut or drastically reduced their funding on the pretext of restraint. The Metis National Council has been reduced to a barebones staff of two. A veteran of that organization commented that "in view of what's happened it's hard to get people excited about the Constitution."

It is here that the cultural and social organizations will prove to be extremely useful to the Metis. They will continue to develop Metis awareness and to educate future leaders for the next round of political talks.

A glimmer of hope appeared at the end of 1987. Georges Erasmus met with federal Justice Minister Ramon Hnatyshyn to discuss the possibility of a further constitutional conference on aboriginal rights. According to reports, they agreed to continue their discussion into 1988. In the meantime, NCC president Louis Bruyere was canvassing provincial premiers about such a possibility. Under his proposal, an agreement in principle would be negotiated prior to the conference being called, with the conference's only purpose being to approve what had been negotiated behind the scenes. In a *Globe and Mail* interview, he indicated that he did not see such a conference taking place until at least 1990. While negotiations would for the most part be out of the public eye, success would not be achieved without a softening of positions on the part of some of the parties concerned.

8
The Future

Canada is at a crossroads in its dealings with the Metis. Looking to the future, there is an optimistic scenario but also a pessimistic one; present developments suggest that we could be heading down either path.

Even if the pessimistic scenario becomes reality, there is one thing Canadians should have learned in the last two hundred years — the Metis will not abandon their struggle. If a satisfactory accommodation is not reached in the next few years, in two or three decades the struggle will regain its momentum.

The Optimistic Scenario

January 29, 2005, La Loche, Saskatchewan. The Northwest Saskatchewan Metis Regional Council is meeting for the first time since its November council elections. The council is the result of a tripartite agreement between the federal government, the Saskatchewan government and the organization representing Saskatchewan Metis. This agreement, signed in 1998 after five years of negotiation, created a regional government for the approximately five thousand Metis of northwest Saskatchewan, who live in an area covering some 18,200 square kilometres and seven communities. While the same area has some non-natives — and nine Indian Reserves (which have their own governments) with a population of some 2,500 people — the vast majority of the people are Metis and non-status Indians. Some of the people in the seven communities are status Indians who have chosen to live off the reserve. In these communities, little distinction is made between Indians, non-status Indians and Metis.

Several contentious issues face the council. First, whether to renew a logging lease granted to the American multinational, IPAC Pulp and Paper Company, which operates a pulp mill several hundred kilometres to the south. Under the terms of its previous logging lease the company agreed that local people would constitute at least 80 per cent of its workforce. It also provided for an annual payment to the council of $1 million.

Some people argue that the community should harvest the logs itself and either set up a sawmill, or alternatively, contract to provide the pulp mill with logs. The other major source of opposition is from the one hundred families who still live by hunting and trapping. These people insist that every year the loggers destroy more of their hunting and trapping grounds and that, unless stopped, logging will destroy their way of life.

Along with these local pressures, the council also has to deal with the provincial government. On several occasions during the late 1980s, area residents blocked logging roads in an attempt to force the government to surrender control over natural resources. The protesters' slogan was "Local Resources for Local People," and while the provincial government was not unsympathetic, it was reluctant to give up its revenue base. Eventually, in 1998, a compromise was reached whereby lands were divided into three categories — a concept that was copied from the 1975 James Bay Agreement.

The council was given absolute jurisdiction over lands immediately surrounding the Metis communities — approximately seven hundred square kilometres, or 4 per cent of the total territory. This land is categorized as Category 1 land and title to it is in the name of the Metis council. A further three thousand square kilometres is category 2 land, over which the local council has authority subject to a provincial veto. The province also retains the right to propose resource-development plans to the council, and an arbitration procedure exists to resolve deadlocks between the province and the council. In category 2 lands, the Saskatchewan government retains 40 per cent of the income earned from resource development. In return for getting 60 per cent of the revenue, the council assumes exclusive responsibility for certain services to people within its geographic area of jurisdiction, including education, social services and health. The province does not provide any money for such services. Finally, category 2 lands are owned by the province; however, the 1998 agreement is constitutionally entrenched, thereby guaranteeing the council control over the land and a share of the revenue arising from it. The IPAC lease involves category 2 land.

The rest of the land — 14,500 square kilometres — is within the absolute control of the province, subject only to local residents having priority over non-residents for the right to hunt and fish. The exercise of this prior right is subject to provincial hunting laws.

The council's jurisdiction over education gives rise to the second contentious issue it has to deal with: language of instruction in the schools. Some parents argue that it should be Cree; others argue that the schools should teach only in English and French; still others argue for English instruction only. And some parents are calling for the teaching of Michif, to ensure that it survives as a language.

Several linguistics experts from the Gabriel Dumont Institute and the newly established Metis Cultural Centre at Batoche are in attendance to provide advice on Metis languages. So, too, are members of the Metis Assembly of Saskatchewan. While this body has no power over the council, it plays an advisory role and tries to coordinate cultural development in Metis communities. It also acts as a lobby group on behalf of Metis interests in Regina and Ottawa.

The two Saskatchewan MLAs representing the Metis in the legislature are also present. Under 1998 amendments to the Saskatchewan Act, the Metis are entitled to two legislative seats. The change to the Saskatchewan Act has been approved by both the provincial legislature and federal Parliament, thus giving it constitutional protection. (The idea for native seats in the legislature was copied from New Zealand, where the Maoris are guaranteed 4 seats in the 97 seat New Zealand Parliament).

Far to the southeast, in Winnipeg, another Metis organization is meeting. The Metis School Board of Greater Winnipeg is in session preparing next year's budget and is having to make hard choices. The board's income — consisting of equalization payments from the Manitoba government, local tax revenue and income from a trust fund set up by court order after the Metis successfully sued the federal and Manitoba governments over land they lost in the 1870s — is insufficient to cover all the programming which the board would like to offer.

The board would like to develop and offer a course in Metis music. It has found two qualified and interested individuals to develop the course. The costs of such a course will be in excess of $200,000 (including teachers' salaries). Already the board has had to close two classrooms in the three schools it operates for budget reasons. And earlier this evening the board decided to save money by dropping its vocational programmes and contracting with the public school system for such classes.

Despite these problems, the Metis of Winnipeg take great pride in their school board and jealously guard its independence. The origins of the board date to the 1990s. Unlike their counterparts in northwest Saskatchewan, the Winnipeg Metis could not set up a government in the midst of their city. Instead, Metis leaders in the 1990s took a look at what areas they considered most important to them. One priority was education — it was a means to ensure the perpetuation of their culture and history. Negotiations with the province — which began in 1988 — were long and hard, but finally, as part of the settlement of the lawsuit begun by the Metis, the provincial government agreed to allow the Metis to have their own schools in areas where "numbers warrant." This was guaranteed by provincial legislation and by an amendment to the Manitoba Act, the province's constitution.

Metis school boards now exist in four areas of the province, including Winnipeg, and are modelled on the separate school system found in many provinces. Individuals living in areas where there is a Metis School Board can elect which school system they choose to support with their education tax dollars. Of course, in these areas it is not compulsory for Metis to support their system, just as it is open for non-Metis to support the Metis system.

Metis schools in the province are supported by the Winnipeg-based Louis Riel Institute, which develops some of the materials used in the system and trains teachers for it. The institute is affiliated with the Faculty of Education at the University of Manitoba.

The Metis education program is the most visible arm of Metis self-government in Manitoba. There are others, however, including a Metis advisory council to the provincial cabinet and a Metis-run development fund, financed by the trust fund set up as part of the settlement of the Metis lawsuit. And like their counterparts in Saskatchewan, the Metis are guaranteed two seats in the Manitoba Legislature.

Problems to Solve

For this fictional scenario to become reality, a number of developments currently underway will have to come to fruition. In particular, the Metis will have to achieve their goal of self-government.

The Metis National Council calls for self-government to be negotiated on a regional level, with such regional governments to be the key units in Metis self-government. According to their vision, there would be a body to coordinate matters of a province-wide nature and a national council to lobby the federal government and international institutions.

On the eve of the 1987 constitutional conference, Saskatchewan premier Grant Devine pointed out how his government had transferred some farmland (approximately twelve hundred hectares) near Lebret to a Metis non-profit corporation, and he indicated his willingness to negotiate the transfer to the Metis of six other government farm operations, all of which had been established in the 1940s to train Metis to be farmers. In March of the same year Saskatchewan's Northern Development Advisory Council recommended the transfer to northern communities of certain Crown lands, government-owned sawmills and such programmes as housing and welfare. It also recommended a sharing of resource revenue earned from northern lands with the communities. Unfortunately, negotiations regarding greater Metis control which started in 1985 broke off in 1987.

The situation is better in Alberta, where the government is proceeding with its new plan for eight Metis settlements and is discussing with the Metis Association of Alberta ways in which Metis communities can have a greater say in services. Elsewhere, as well, the pace of negotiating has picked up. In Manitoba, tripartite negotiations involving the federal and provincial governments and the Manitoba Metis Federation have begun with a view to granting greater powers over housing, education, economic development and family services to Metis communities. At a joint news conference in January 1988, the three parties to the negotiations called this the first step on the road to Metis self-government in Manitoba. The province and the Metis also announced a plan to establish an independent Metis educational institute, to be called the Louis Riel Institute. In Ontario, preliminary discussions have been held to develop a negotiation process for off-reserve native people.

Apart from government resistance, the biggest obstacle to the realization of Metis hopes is financial. Most Metis communities operate at the poverty-level and therefore do not have a population which can be taxed. In order for a government to be effective, it must have an economic base. For Metis communities, this can be achieved in one of three ways. First, economic development schemes could be established which will give rise to a tax base. For such economic development to occur, government-provided capital would have to be injected into the communities. Second, provincial and federal governments could surrender control of some resource income to Metis communities; they could, for example, turn over the ownership of minerals in an area. The third way would be by direct annual transfers from Ottawa and the provinces.

The last option is one already exercised by the federal government in other areas: it transfers money to the provinces to fund welfare, education, hospitalization and medicare. Ottawa also makes equalization payments to have-not provinces. If equalization is guaranteed for the have-not provinces, there is no reason why it should not also be guaranteed for native governments which may be set up in the future.

Even if financial hurdles are overcome — a big "if" in this age of fiscal restraint — other obstacles remain.

Local communities will have to be trained in exercising self-government. Clem Chartier admits that there is a lot of community education work to do before the Metis form their regional governments. He suggests that time has to be spent in the communities talking about self-government, how it can be put into place and what the implications are for local people. But even if aboriginal self-government were immediately accepted by all levels of government, there would still be. a long period of development. Governments do not spring up overnight. Ideas will have to be tried and negotiations undertaken with provincial and neighbouring municipal governments. For self-government to work, in many instances aboriginal communities will have to join together to share the cost of a service. In other cases, contracts will have to be entered into with neighbouring municipalities and provinces to provide services. Canadians often ask: what does self-government mean? The answer: it is an evolutionary process whereby, through trial and error, native communities will take greater responsibility for matters directly affecting their communities. It should be remembered that in 1867 no one could have predicted what kind of Canada would evolve, just as today no one can predict what the Meech Lake Accord will mean for the country.

What powers should such a native government have? Should it be a provincial style of government, should it adopt a municipal government model or should an entirely new order of government be developed? What authority should it have over non-Metis living in its area of jurisdiction? There are no easy answers to such questions. Canadians must accept that there is not a single definition of self-government which will be acceptable to all native communities in Canada. Because of differences in climate, available resources, populations and location relative to major urban centres, the form of self-government will vary. What the Inuit on Baffin Island need will not necessarily work for the Metis settlements in Alberta. It is for that reason that Canada's aboriginal groups call for the implementation of self-government on a regional basis.

The Pessimistic Scenario

The pessimistic scenario is much easier to paint than the optimistic one. It is at best the status quo and at worse a much grimmer economic and social picture for Canada's Metis people. There are many reasons to believe that politically Canada is back in 1885. The constitutional talks have failed. In addition, at neither the constitutional talks nor elsewhere have the Metis had any success in gaining a land base. Things may change, but at the moment governments are showing little desire to take a more generous stance on native rights.

The Metis are in a worse position than other native peoples. In spite of the collapse of the constitutional talks, devolution of power from the federal Department of Indian Affairs to individual Indian bands is continuing. Some 60 to 70 per cent of Canada's Indian people still live on reserves. Here they function as a homogeneous community with the right to practise their culture and a place where they can speak their language. Even without the devolution of power, the band councils have some say in reserve affairs. Further, reserves are protected against large-scale intrusion by non-natives.

The Inuit are in a similar position to the Indians. While they do not have reserves, they live in parts of the country where they form the overwhelming majority of the population, and they have been able to protect their culture and language. Talks are proceeding, though slowly, on the creation of Nunavut, an Inuit-run government.

Both the Inuit and certain Indian groups are actively negotiating land claims with the federal government. If the models of the James Bay Agreement and the 1984 Western Arctic Agreement are followed, future land claims agreements will likely include at least some measure of self-government for the native people affected.

The Metis, on the other hand, have little cause to be excited about the future of self-government. While talks have been underway in Alberta, Saskatchewan, Manitoba and Ontario on transfer of land and control to Metis communities, they are still at a preliminary stage, and in some cases, notably Saskatchewan's, they have come to a standstill. This is a dangerous situation for the Metis, because they are not shielded from outside influences to the same extent as are the Indians and Inuit. Without a geographic area where they can exercise some measure of control, the Metis might find their survival threatened.

And there are other grounds for worry. With national and provincial debts growing at alarming rates, governments are starting to cut back their financial assistance to native peoples. In 1987 the federal government ended its $1 million annual grant to the Metis National Council for constitutional development. The Saskatchewan government eliminated its 1987 grant of $750,000 to the Association of Metis and Non-Status Indians of Saskatchewan. Saskatchewan also eliminated its 1987 grant to the Native Courtworker Program which operated out of the Friendship Centres.

What does all this mean? For some Metis, it will mean the end of their dream of breaking out of a cycle of poverty. Resentment will grow. It will grow until it reaches a breaking point as in 1869, 1885, the 1930s in Alberta and the 1960s. In the meantime, institutions like the Friendship Centres and the Gabriel Dumont Institute will play an important role in keeping alive the idea of a Metis society.

The Metis in the Northwest Territories

The Northwest Territories, with a population of five thousand Metis, is one area of the country where the optimistic scenario may become reality in the near future.

In the NWT, status under the Indian Act has not separated the Indian people from other natives to the same extent as in other areas of Canada, in part because there are no Indian reserves in the Territories (many rights of Indian people are directly tied to reserves). As a result, Metis and Indians in the NWT have worked closely together to achieve common goals. Not only have the Dene Indians and the Metis joined together — after some encouragement from Ottawa — to negotiate a land claims settlement with the federal government, but they have cooperated in working for the division of the Territories into an Inuit province and a province composed of Dene, Metis and non-natives.

In a 1982 plebiscite, 56 per cent of the Territories' voters approved the idea of a division. The division of the territories was also approved by the federal government on condition that a boundary be agreed upon between the Inuit and the Dene/Metis. In the fall of 1982 the Dene/

Metis formed the Western Constitutional Forum to consult with their people on the development of a proposal for their government. The Inuit formed a similar group called the Nunavut Constitutional Forum.

Under the proposal of the Western Constitutional Forum, the Dene/Metis territory — covering most of the western Territories south and west of the treeline — would become Denendeh. It would include a sizeable non-native population and such centres as Yellowknife. Since the majority of the population — 57 per cent — would be non-native, the proposal includes guarantees to ensure the survival of the Dene/Metis. Denendeh would have power over fisheries and navigable waters (currently under federal jurisdiction) to ensure adequate protection of the environment — something that is essential if the native way of life is to be maintained. Employment and labour would also be solely under Denendeh jurisdiction. Native languages would be entrenched in the provincial constitution and some decisions would have to be approved by community assemblies (the process used to develop their proposals). Native people would be guaranteed a minimum of 30 per cent of all legislative and town council seats. A native senate would have the power to veto all legislation which adversely affected aboriginal rights. In part, these provisions stem from the lesson learned by the Metis in Manitoba during the 1870s, when they lost control of the province they helped create.

Different cultural groups could form their own regional municipalities. In some areas of jurisdiction these municipalities would be semi-autonomous. Regional municipalities could designate English and a native language as official languages. The proposal initially called for a ten-year residency requirement for voting so as to ensure that the government stayed in the hands of long-term residents. The lengthy residence requirement has come under considerable criticism and may be modified.

The Inuit too, have been busy preparing a proposal for their own province — Nunavut. Their proposal can be summed up as follows. Essentially the Inuit propose a provincial form of government, with a legislative assembly having the kinds of powers that southern legislatures possess. But they also propose that their government have some jurisdiction in foreign affairs. Primarily, they want to ensure that they will be able to maintain contact with Inuit who live in other parts of the world, such as Greenland, Alaska and the Soviet Union. Inuktitut would be one of the official languages. Finally, they propose a three-year residency requirement for voting.

One of the big stumbling blocks in dividing the Territories has been the boundary question. Initially, the Inuit proposed that the treeline should form the border. This would have placed the Mackenzie Delta-Beaufort Sea area (including Aklavik, Inuvik and Tuktoyaktuk) in Nunavut. The 2,500 Inuvialuit of this area share language and culture with the eastern Inuit (though they are believed to have arrived in Canada much more recently than their eastern counterparts), but their economic and transportation system is tied to the western NWT. The Dene/ Metis wanted this area in their jurisdiction because the Mackenzie River was part of their transportation system and because of the oil in the area. The area was the subject of a land claims agreement reached in 1984 between Ottawa and the Inuvialuit.

At length, agreement was reached that the Inuvialuit should be in Denendeh. The regional semi-autonomous municipalities proposed by the Western Constitutional Forum would be a means of ensuring that the Inuvialuit could preserve their language and culture. However, the Inuvialuit did not consent to this agreement, and according to recent reports they are reserving the right to decide in which jurisdiction they would like to be included. In January 1987, a tentative agreement on the boundary issue was reached by the Inuit and Dene/Metis negotiators. A plebiscite on the boundary was to have been held in May of that year, and had it been approved the Territories were slated for division in 1991.

But the agreement was not approved by some of the constituent groups and the accord fell apart. Ways are being sought to resolve the impasse. Federal arbitration has been suggested if the parties cannot resolve the dispute themselves. The major issue in the dispute is a strip of land extending northward from the Saskatchewan-Manitoba border. The Dogrib and Sahtu Indians are claiming part of the territory in the Contwoyto Lake area which is also claimed by the Kitikmeot Inuit. Also at issue is management of the cariboo herd in the Thelon Game Sanctuary, directly north of the Saskatchewan-Manitoba border. Talks were to resume in 1988, though many observers expressed pessimism as to whether they would.

If division is reached on a boundary line, the question will then be whether the two new governments should become provinces. Here the constitution becomes important. Prior to 1982, Ottawa could have unilaterally created new provinces, as it did in 1905 by creating Alberta and Saskatchewan. After the adoption of the 1982 Constitution, the creation of a new province required the consent of Ottawa and seven provinces with 50 per cent of the population. Under the Meech Lake Accord, all ten provinces must agree.

According to Gordon Robertson, a former Clerk of the Privy Council and Cabinet Secretary for Federal-Provincial Affairs, obtaining the unanimous consent of the provinces will likely be impossible. The reason involves the constitutionally entrenched equalization scheme, under which payments are based on per-capita tax-yield. In his study for The Institute for Research on Public Policy, *Northern Provinces: a mistaken goal*, Robertson points out that the tax-yield in the NWT is above the national average, and so disqualifies future northern provinces from receiving equalization payments. However, because of the high cost of governing (small population in a large territory, high costs of transportation and goods), the tax yield is not sufficient to support the government. Massive financial support from Ottawa is required. Robertson therefore argues that it is unlikely ten provinces would agree to an equalization formula which would treat two provinces (Nunavut and Denendah) more favourably than other provinces. As an alternative, he suggests the creation, by federal and territorial legislation, of autonomous federal territories with full self-governing powers. He believes that the constitution could be amended to approve such entities.

Why Self-Government?

The prospect of Metis self-government in the north and elsewhere must be viewed realistically. Some people see self-government as a panacea for all the social problems facing the Metis. Such a vision is an unfortunate one and probably does more harm than good to the cause.

Self-government will not suddenly empty the prison cells of Metis; nor will it instantly transform the Metis people from have-nots to haves. Metis self-government may or may not change the economic well-being of the people. Policy errors will be made and native governments will undoubtedly indulge in their share of patronage and even corruption. Native governments, however, should not be judged by a higher standard than non-native governments. Unfortunately, patronage, incompetence and occasional corruption are also a fact of non-native governments. One could easily fill a chapter of this book listing examples of blatant patronage, incompetence and criminal acts by Canada's elected politicians during the last year. What self-government means is the right to be wrong.

Undoubtedly, some members unhappy with the actions of their Metis government will challenge the authority of their leadership through the non-native court system. Often the Charter of Rights and Freedoms will be their weapon. The American experience with Indian self-government is instructive. In the United States, interventions by the federal courts are a regular occurrence in the operations of Indian governments on reserves. The regularity of such interventions has, in fact, become a source of dispute between Indian people and the federal government, with Indian tribal governments complaining that the courts have too much power over them. A whole body of judicial precedents on when courts can and cannot intervene in the operations of Indian government has developed. Hundreds of lawyers have specialized in this area of the law alone. Matters were further complicated when in 1968 Congress passed the Indian Civil Rights Act requiring Indian governments to guarantee certain minimum standards in judicial proceedings.

Court interventions in Canada would not be unique to Metis governments, they are already a fact of life in non-native governments. Municipal elections have been quashed for irregularity, while provincial Sunday closing laws and federal abortion laws have been struck down. Canada's Charter of Rights has given the courts an even larger role in reviewing the actions of governments. There is little reason to believe that native governments will be exempt from such scrutiny.

Self-government does not mean independence from Canada; in fact, no Metis leaders have advocated such a position. Rather, self-government means the Metis having a say in matters directly affecting their communities. It also means having a say in the terms under which they will be a part of the greater Canadian union. To achieve this goal, discussions will be necessary to incorporate self-government and other Metis aspirations into the Constitution.

Accommodating Metis aspirations in the Constitution is not a radical idea. One of Canada's strengths has been its ability to accept different cultures and peoples into the federation. The Constitution needs to evolve and grow to accommodate different needs. It is not a static instrument locking Canadians forever into a particular mold. Confederation and the Constitution have grown to accommodate the French fact in Canada, there is now a greater awareness of Canada's multicultural character, and the principle of sexual equality has been enshrined in the Constitution. In light of all this, recognizing Metis aspirations in the Constitution should be seen as a welcome, exciting development. Institutions which do not grow become stale and die.

Self-government is important to the Metis for cultural preservation. While officially Canada is a multicultural country, that is no guarantee of cultural survival for any of its ethnic groups. The children of immigrants are rapidly assimilated into the English-French milieu; French-Canadians outside Quebec are hard-pressed to preserve their language and culture. To ward off the threat of assimilation, control over schools, public services and economic development is essential. This is a lesson that Quebec has learned well, and it underlies the Metis' drive for self-government.

Since history has shown that Metis claims will not go away, Canada should deal with them now. If it does not, in another twenty or thirty years the Metis' grievances will surface again, perhaps in a violent form. With education (today there are at least thirty Metis lawyers in Canada; twenty years ago there were none) Metis leaders will become more aware of their rights and more effective in advancing their cause. They will point to the Constitution which recognizes the Metis as one of the aboriginal peoples of Canada. They will want to know what that means. They will ask Canada to finish its constitutional business. Those who hope for the assimilation of the Metis may be in for a long wait.

Selected Bibliography

Books

Adams, Howard. *Prison of Grass*. Toronto: General Publishing, 1975

Barron, F. Laurie and Waldram, James B. eds. *1885 And After: Native Society in Transition*. Regina: University of Regina, Canadian Plains Research Center, 1986

Berger, Thomas R. *Fragile Freedoms: Human Rights and Dissent in Canada*. Toronto: Irwin Publishing, Inc., 1982

Boldt, Menno and Long, Anthony J. eds. *The Quest for Justice: Aboriginal Peoples and Aboriginal Rights*. Toronto: The University of Toronto Press, 1985

Brown, Jennifer S. and Peterson, Jacqueline, ed. *The New Peoples, Being and Becoming Métis in North America*. Winnipeg: University of Manitoba Press, 1985

Campbell, Maria. *Half-Breed*. Toronto: McClelland and Stewart, 1973

Daniels, Harry W., ed. *The Forgotten People, Metis and non-status Indian Land Claims*. Ottawa: Native

Council of Canada, 1979

Dobbin, Murray. *The One-And-A-Half Men*. Vancouver: New Star Books, 1981

Douaud, Patrick C. *Ethnolinguistic Profile of the Canadian Metis*. Ottawa: National Museum of Man Mercury Series, 1985

Eisler, Dale. *Rumours of Glory: Saskatchewan & the Thatcher Years*. Edmonton: Hurtig Publishers, 1987

Flanagan, Thomas. *Riel and the Rebellion: 1885 Reconsidered*. Saskatoon: Western Producer Prairie Books, 1983

Frideres, James S. *Native People in Canada, Contemporary Conflicts* (2nd ed.). Scarborough: Prentice-Hall Canada, Inc, 1983

Friesen, Gerald. *The Canadian Prairies*. Toronto: University of Toronto Press, 1984

Getty, Ian A.L. and Lussier, Antoine S., ed., *As Long as the Sun Shines and Water Flows, A Reader In Canadian Native Studies*. Vancouver: University of British Columbia Press, 1983

Giraud, Marcel, George Woodcock, trans. *The Métis in the Canadian West*, Volumes I and II. Edmonton: The University of Alberta Press, 1986

Hildebrandt, Walter. *The Battle of Batoche: British Small Warfare and the Entrenched Métis*. Ottawa: Parks Canada, 1985

MacEwan, Grant. *Metis Makers of History*. Saskatoon: Western Producer Prairie Books, 1981

MacGregor, James G. *Father Lacombe*. Edmonton: Hurtig Publishers, 1975

McLean, Don. *1885: Metis Rebellion or Government*

Conspiracy? Winnipeg: Pemmican Publications, 1985

Metis Association of Alberta; Ferguson, Theresa; Sawchuk, Joe and Patricia. *Metis Land Rights in Alberta: A Political History.* Edmonton: Metis Association of Alberta, 1981

Morton, Desmond (author of the introduction). *The Queen v.Louis Riel.* Toronto: The University of Toronto Press, 1974

Newman, Peter C. *Company of Adventurers.* Markham: Penguin Books of Canada, 1985

Payment, Diane. *Batoche (1870-1910).* Saint-Boniface: Les Editions du Blé, 1983

Ray, Arthur J. *Indians in the Fur Trade.* Toronto: University of Toronto Press, 1974

Redbird, Duke. *We Are Metis, A Metis View of the Development of a Native Canadian People.* Willowdale: Ontario Metis & Non-Status Indian Association, 1980

Robertson, Gordon. *Northern Provinces: a mistaken goal.* Montreal: The Institute for Research on Public Policy, 1985

Romanow, Roy; Whyte, John and Leeson, Howard. *Canada...Nothwithstanding: The Making of the Constitution 1976-1982.* Toronto: Carswell/ Methuen, 1984

Sawchuk, Joe. *The Metis of Manitoba, Reformulation of an Ethnic Identity.* Toronto: Peter Martin Associates Limited, 1978

Schwartz, Bryan. *First Principles, Second Thoughts: Aboriginal Peoples, Constitutional Reform and Canadian Statecraft.* Montreal: The Institute for

Research on Public Policy, 1986

Sealey, D. Bruce and Lussier, Antoine S. *The Métis: Canada's Forgotten People*. Winnipeg: Pemmican Publications, 1975

Government Reports

Native Affairs Secretariat. *Alberta's Metis Settlements: A Compendium of Background Documents*. Edmonton: Native Affairs Secretariat, 1984

Report of the Royal Commission on the condition of the Halfbreed Population of the Province of Alberta; Government of Alberta, 1936

The Report of the Metis Task Force Upon The Metis Betterment Act, Metis Settlements and the Metis Rehabilitation Branch; Government of Alberta, 1972

Report of the MacEwan Joint Metis-Government Committee to Review the Metis Betterment Act and Regulations. Edmonton: Alberta Minister of Municipal Affairs, 1984

Implementation of Resolution 18. Edmonton: Alberta Municipal Affairs, 1987

Articles, Monographs and Non-government Reports

Alberta Federation of Metis Settlement Associations. "By Means of Conferences and Negotiations We Ensure Our Rights". Edmonton: 1986

Bartlett, Richard. *Subjugation, Self-Management, and Self-Government of Aboriginal Lands and Re-*

sources. Kingston: Institute of Intergovernmental Relations, Queen's University, 1986

Cowie, Ian B. *Future Issues of Jurisdiction and Coordination Between Aboriginal and Non-Aboriginal Governments*. Kingston: Institute of Intergovernmental Relations, Queen's University, 1987

Hatt, Ken. "Ethnic Discourse in Alberta: Land and the Metis in the Ewing Commission." Canadian Ethnic Studies, XVII, 2, 85

McNeil, Kent. *Native Claims in Rupert's Land and the North-Western Territory: Canada's Constitutional Obligations*. Saskatoon: University of Saskatchewan Native Law Centre, 1982

Robertson, Gordon. "Innovation North of Sixty." May 1987 Policy Options Politiques 9

Sawchuk, Joe. "The Metis, Non-Status Indians and the New Aboriginality: Government Influence of Native Political Alliances and Identity." Canadian Ethnic Studies, XVII, 2, 85

Sprague, D.N.. "Government Lawlessness in the Administration of Manitoba Land Claims, 1870-1887." [1980] 10 Manitoba Law Journal (no. 4) 415

Weaver, Sally. "Federal Policy-Making for Metis and non-status Indians in the Context of Native Policy." Canadian Ethnic Studies, XVII, 2, 85

Weinstein, John. "Aboriginal Self-Determination Off A Land Base". Kingston: Institute of Intergovernmental Relations, Queen's University, 1986

Young, Kay and Skarsgard, Anne. "Alberta's Metis Settlement Associations: A Legislative History". Saskatoon: University of Saskatchewan Native Law Centre, 1983

Zlotkin, Norman K. "The 1983 and 1984 Constitutional Conferences: Only the Beginning". (1984) 3 Canadian Native Law Reporter 1

Zlotkin, Norman K. "Unfinished Business: Aboriginal Peoples and the 1983 Constitutional Conference". Kingston: Institute of Intergovernmental Relations, Queen's University, 1983

Court Decisions

Guerin v. The Queen (1985) 1 Canadian Native Law Reporter 120

The Hamlet of Baker Lake v. The Minister of Indian Affairs and Northern Development (1979) 3 Canadian Native Law Reporter 17

L'Hirondelle v. The King, 4 Canadian Native Law Cases 259

L'Hirondelle v. The King, 4 Canadian Native Law Cases 262

Patterson v. Lane, 3 Canadian Native Law Cases 217

Poitras v. Attorney-General of Alberta, (1969) 68 Western Weekly Reports 224

Wright v. Battley, 3 Canadian Native Law Cases 659

Community Histories

Je me Souviens, Histoire de Saint-Louis et des Environs

East Prairie Metis, 1939-1979, 40 Years of Determination

The Press

News stories in the native media were also of considerable help in researching this book. In particular I would like to mention:

Windspeaker, published by Aboriginal Multi-Media Society of Alberta

Kanai News, published by Communications Society of Indian News at Standoff, Alberta

Native Press, published by Native Communications Society of the Western Northwest Territories

New Breed, voice of the Saskatchewan Metis and Non-Status Indians

I also relied on news reports in the *Globe and Mail*, *Saskatoon Star-Phoenix* and the *Winnipeg Free Press*.

Lectures

Berger, Thomas R. "The Manitoba Metis Lawsuit." Victoria: August 22, 1987

Chartier, Clem. "Process of Negotiations for Native Rights." Saskatoon: March 18, 1987

McNeil, Kent. "The Constitution Act, 1982, Sections 25 and 35." Banff: November 22-27, 1987

Ray, Arthur J. "Fur Trade History as an Aspect of Native History: The Early and Late Fur Trade." Saskatoon: February 5, 1987

Sprague, Douglas. "Metis Rights in Western Canada." Saskatoon: January 14, 1983

Index